D1097370

FOCUSED

Reclaim Your Time, Ditch Overwhelm, and Do Less Better

MEGAN FLATT

Copyright © 2023 by Megan Flatt.

All rights reserved. No part of this publication may be reproduced, distributed or transmitted in any form or by any means, including photocopying, recording, or other electronic or mechanical methods, without the prior written permission of the publisher, except in the case of brief quotations embodied in critical reviews and certain other non- © commercial uses permitted by copyright law.

For permission requests, write to the author, at:
hello@letscollective.co

Author Name: Megan Flatt
Typesetting & Cover Design: ndg creative
Publisher Name: Let's Collective
Contact Information:
Let's Collective/Focus Sessions
3030 Bridgeway, Suite 208
Sausalito, Ca
94965

Focused: Reclaim your time, ditch overwhelm, do less better / Megan Flatt—1st ed. **ISBN 979-8-9851082-0-0**

PRAISE FOR *FOCUSED*

"Megan distilled ideas I've heard before in such an approachable and effective way that they finally clicked in my brain. Because of Megan, I'm already making changes to my workday and I'm feeling less anxious and stressed. I have more time than I realize, and it feels empowering to truly focus."

- Jen Rofé, Literary Entrepreneur

"We all know we need to focus, but Megan takes the time to explain why, and then HOW to do it! She has packed decades of personal and professional experience, and the science behind it, into one book. If you're ready to quit hustling and start focusing, you need this book."

- Stacy Spensley, Parenting Coach

"This book changed the way that I think about productivity. The system is easy to follow (even for my easily distracted ADHD brain!) and relies on self-compassion, not shame. Highly recommend! "

- Meg Casebolt, Author and Founder of Love at First Search

"I wasn't sure that actually focusing was possible with all the things going on around me, but this book and Focus Sessions show me it is. I'm using the techniques Megan shares to get super clear on what I want to focus on big picture and day to day — then to actually make the time and focus on those things. I'm getting more done with less overwhelm. Get Focused!"

– Sara Barry, Content Strategist & Coach

First and foremost this book is dedicated to my family, Erik, Brady, and Rylan.

You are my Why.

You are the reason I work to be focused, so I can claim my time with you three, and make an impact on you and on this world for you.

This book is also dedicated to you, the reader. You are meant to do amazing things in this world. You are meant to make an impact. Your family and the world need what you have to offer.

So go out and do your Most Important Work. For them. For all of us.

TABLE OF CONTENTS

Praise for *Focused* iii
Foreword by Grace Kraaijvanger ix
Introduction xiii

PART I:
YOU DON'T NEED MORE TIME, YOU NEED MORE FOCUS

1. Let's Reject Hustle Culture 3
2. You Were Meant to Make an Impact 11
3. Build the House You Want to Live In 23
4. Why You Can't Focus — And Why You Need To 39

PART II:
IS YOUR TO-DO LIST SABOTAGING YOUR PRODUCTIVITY? – WHAT TO FOCUS ON

5. The Art of A Well-Crafted To-Do List 49
6. The Importance of Visioning and Planning 57
7. Make Time for Deep Work 67
8. Clearing the Deck for Focus 77

PART III:
YOU HAVE EXACTLY THE TIME YOU NEED – FINDING TIME TO FOCUS

9. Get Realistic About Time 85
10. Define Your Container 97
11. Your Unique Focus Formula 109
12. Set Up a Schedule That Works for You 127
13. Protecting Distraction-Free Time 143

PART IV:
FIND YOUR FOCUS FLOW — HOW TO FOCUS

14. Hack Your Brain for Focus 155
15. Create Your Own Flow for Focus 163
16. Celebrate, Adjust, and Build on Your Momentum 173

PART V:
WHEN FOCUS GETS TOUGH, RAISE YOUR RESILIENCE

17. When There Is Just Too Much To Do 181
18. When There Are Too Many Choices 191
19. When Others Disrupt Your Flow 199
20. When You Are Just Overwhelmed 207

Acknowledgements xix
References & Resources xxi
About the Author xxiii
Bonus Materials xxiv

FOREWORD

In a world where distractions are abundant and attention spans are short, it's an understatement to say that it's difficult for visionary entrepreneurs to stay focused on the task at hand. When we feel overwhelmed and unfocused, we lose confidence. We forget what we're selling, who it's for, or why we started this business in the first place. Feeling overwhelmed is more than an uncomfortable emotion; it puts at peril our hard work to build a business we believe in. Megan Flatt's simple and effective strategies reign us back in from "trying to do all of the things" back into a zone of clarity and remembering the deeper, more important "why" that got us here in the first place.

How could I have known when I met Megan almost 10 years ago that we would become collaborators, business besties, and that she'd be by my side helping me make countless decisions for my business? Megan has helped me reconnect with with my mission when I experienced burnout, partnered with me to share her tools and expertise to thousands of creative women entrepreneurs, and taught her kind yet clear strategies for focusing on what brings joy and revenue to those of us who wear the hat of creative, intentional, soulful business owner.

Megan has been mentoring and teaching women entrepreneurs for over a decade to create work and professional offerings that align with their zone of genius. Megan practices what she preaches and is truly working squarely and consistently in her zone of genius. She teaches us how to focus during a time that small business owners are in a torrential deluge of advice, ideas, and strategies for how to grow our businesses.

Megan was a trail-blazer in realizing that successful entrepreneurship for women isn't about know-how or connections or having fancy business degrees, but about focus. Megan knew that if she could offer women entrepreneurs clarity, focus, and accountability, that she could change the trajectory of their business. And that she has done for thousands of founders like me and those in The Hivery community. I trust Megan's approach implicitly, and I'm thrilled that this book is in your hands so that you can be armed with the tools and loving, brilliant tips that Megan has been supporting me and my community with all along.

Armed with her signature Post-its, I have participated in countless trainings, classes, and Focus Sessions. Megan knows how to cut through the clutter of the monkey mind of ideas, opportunities, and to-do items and helps us to focus on the most important issues of the moment. Whether that's revenue, product clarity, raising prices, or knowing who we're selling to, Megan knows how to get us focused and out of overwhelm like no other. You, my friend, are in for a great adventure of focus and planning that will give you the exhale you've been looking for during your journey of entrepreneurship, whether you're just getting started or you're a seasoned business owner.

Inside this book you'll find practical tips and strategies for developing and maintaining focus in your daily work, as well as insights from successful entrepreneurs who have mastered the art of staying focused. But this book is more than a collection of tips and anecdotes. It's a powerful reminder that focus is not just a nice-to-have skill for small business owners — it's an essential ingredient for success.The ability to stay focused on your goals, prioritize your time, and tune out distractions can make all the difference in achieving your dreams.

So if you're ready to take your small business to the next level, I encourage you to dive into this book with an open mind and a willingness to learn from my friend, mentor, and collaborator, Megan Flatt. I have no doubt that you'll come away with a renewed sense of purpose and commitment to staying focused on what really matters...you and your brilliant business. Grab your Post-its. You're about to go on a planning and focus adventure with my dear and wisdom-filled friend, Megan Flatt.

Grace Kraaijvanger

Founder, The Hivery

http://TheHivery.com

INTRODUCTION

Hi there, Entrepreneur. I know you.

You have great ideas, world-changing ideas. You already know you are meant to make an impact. In fact, you probably are already changing the lives of those around you. I also know: You are busy. You constantly add more to your to-do list and your goal sheet. You work harder, you put in more effort, and you frequently feel like you should be getting more done.

You aren't alone. A survey conducted by Udemy, an online learning platform, found that 63% of American workers feel like they don't work as efficiently as they could. And RescueTime, a time tracking software, found that 79% of survey respondents said they want to be more productive at work, and that distractions and interruptions are a major obstacle to productivity.

And it's not just about getting distracted. When surveyed, business owners in our Focus Sessions community said the number one thing holding them back in their business was too much to do and not enough time to do it.

We also live in a culture that promotes constant hustle and accomplishment at all costs. We are bombarded with messages to do more, do better, do it all.

But what if it's not about doing more. more. more, but what if it was actually around doing less? And not just doing less and, therefore, achieving less. What if we did less, but did it better?

What if we were more impactful in our work, relationships, and day-to-day actions? What if we celebrated our wins, rather than constantly beating ourselves up for what we haven't done? What if we could start our days feeling empowered rather than frazzled, and end our days feeling accomplished rather than disappointed?

I believe we can.

In 2021, I launched a program called Focus Sessions. Focus Sessions provides dedicated, distraction-free, virtual coworking to busy entrepreneurs just like you. These hosted sessions bring together people from all over the world to find their Focus Flow and get their Most Important Work done all in a supportive, inclusive community.

Members in our community are more focused and are achieving more. They have started new businesses; they are writing memoirs; they are increasing revenue while decreasing the time they spend working. Becoming more focused is helping our members prioritize their personal wellness, their families, and the things that matter most to them. You'll read about some of these members in this book. (We'd love to have you join us. Check out http://focus-sessions.com/bookbonus for more information, plus printable copies of all the worksheets in the book for you to fill out for yourself.)

As you read, we are going to find out how to reclaim your time, do less better, and actually get things done without overwhelm and burnout.

We'll uncover why focus is hard to access, especially now, and how you can use brain science to work more efficiently instead of working more.You'll discover how to detox your calendar, prioritize the right tasks, and stop letting your to-do list actually sabotage your productivity.

Plus you'll learn how to get out of nonstop overwhelm.

By the end of this book, you'll know how to break the productivity-shame cycle and make a bigger impact with your work, without burning out.

It's not going to be easy or an overnight fix — you have been operating this way for 20, 40, or 60 years — but you deserve it. And the world deserves your genius when you can show up in a way that is complete, authentic, and let's face it, not exhausted.

This book is meant to be your guide. So read, learn, and most of all: pause and take action. Use the exercises, worksheets, and prompts in this book to help you make meaningful change. And revisit these action steps. You don't have to do everything in the book or change everything in your life and business in one fell swoop; take what resonates with you and leave the rest. Come back to these options any time you need to make an adjustment in your life or business.

Why? Because the world needs your Most Important Work.

Let's get started!

PART I

YOU DON'T NEED MORE TIME, YOU NEED MORE FOCUS

“The idea of Hustle Culture is based on the notion that more is always better and that rest is for the weak.”

Lisa Bodell

CHAPTER 1:

LET'S REJECT HUSTLE CULTURE

I have always been a lover of productivity and time management, and I have spent years using those skills to help entrepreneurs make more money, especially women and underrepresented groups. The problem was that a lot of conversations, especially around being a successful entrepreneur, stemmed around hustle as a key strategy. The idea that we had to work harder, work longer, work to the edge of burnout if we wanted to reach our goals was everywhere. In fact, when I googled "quotes around entrepreneurship" a few of the first ones that popped up were "success requires sacrifice," "entrepreneurs never sleep," and even plainly, "embrace the hustle."

Even as a productivity expert, a few years ago I found I was going down that path myself. If I worked a little harder, a little longer — if I just sacrificed a little more — I'd get the success I was chasing. (Nevermind that I never stopped long enough to celebrate the success I already had attained!) Was I successful? Yes. I hit revenue goals, I was honored for achievements, and I was getting stuff DONE.

But I also hit a wall. I was working all the time, but I wasn't excited about the work I used to love. I went to bed exhausted and woke up just as tired. I'd finish my day and still feel like there were infinite tasks on my to-do list, and it left me listless and resentful. To put it simply: I was burned out. But I didn't know it yet. Afterall, I was a mom, a business owner, a volunteer in my community, there was unrest in the world that needed attention....we were ALL busy, right? I thought if I planned better, if I structured my time better, I'd be able to get it all done. If I just hustled a little harder, it would all fall into place.

> *"Rejecting hustle culture means recognizing that burnout is not a badge of honor."* —*Jocelyn K Glei*

I realized there had to be a better way.

Doing more wasn't working. Multitasking wasn't working. I needed to do less, but do less better. I needed to get really clear on how and where I could make the biggest impact, in my life and on those around me, and I needed to double down there. There are plenty of people (usually cis-het white men without kids or who are not the primary caregiver) telling us how to use our time, but for most of us who are socialized as women, assigned female at birth, or part of another marginalized community, there are many more layers. I needed to take what I knew about time management and productivity, and assess what was working for me as an entrepreneur who was also taking care of other people.

I thought about when I felt the best in my work and in my life, and I asked others what worked for them. It all came down to some form of focus.

Hustle culture wasn't working. Let me rephrase that. **Hustle culture doesn't work. It's time to stop wearing Hustle Culture like a badge of honor. It is time to embrace Focus Culture.**

What is **Focus Culture** and how is it different from Hustle Culture? Let's look at them side by side.

Instead of this **Hustle Culture** *fallacy...*	→	*...try this* **Focus Culture** *re-frame!*
I need more time.	→	**I have exactly the time I need.**
Do more!	→	**Do less better.**
No pain, no gain.	→	**Focus is self-care.**
Burnout is inevitable.	→	**Burnout is not a badge of honor.**
Make it epic.	→	**Make it repeatable.**
How do we get more done?	→	**How do we simplify?**
I'm so busy!	→	**I am in charge of my day.**
Get more done.	→	**Get the right things done.**
Be more productive.	→	**Be more focused and efficient.**
Success is all about me.	→	**You don't have to do it alone.**

Hustle culture tells us to do more and work harder at all costs. Hustle culture tells us that we are at the mercy of our calendar, the clock and capitalism. Hustle culture controls us. Focus Culture puts us back in charge.

Hustle culture says, "I need more time," but Focus Culture says, "I have exactly the time I need." This was the phrase that really started it all for me. I would wake up at three in the morning, panicking about all of the things that I needed to get done, not only in my business, but for my kids and my family and in my community and all of the things that I wanted to do, but felt like I didn't have time for. When I woke up like this, I would put my hand on my chest and remind myself, "I have exactly the time I need." That is the crux of what started this idea of Focus Culture.

Hustle Culture has a narrow definition of success. With Focus Culture, you decide what your top priorities are and where you spend your energy. Focus culture puts you in charge of your day. And it turns out, when you are more focused, you actually tend to get more done. Trying to do more doesn't make you more productive, but improving your focus can.

Hustle and burnout should not be seen as the norm for entrepreneurs, but rather as a warning sign that our approach to work and life needs to be reevaluated. So let's reject these Hustle Culture relics: needing more time; doing more, more, more; no pain, no gain; burnout; the pressure to be epic; figuring out how to get more done; being too busy; celebrating doing more; going it alone.

It's time to embrace the new Focus Culture affirmations:

- I have exactly the time I need.
- Do less better.
- Focus is self-care.
- Make it repeatable.
- Let's simplify.
- I am in charge of my day.
- Let's get the right things done.
- Be focused and efficient.
- You don't have to do it alone.

Which one resonates most with you?

Grab a Post-it note, write it down for yourself, and stick it somewhere you can see it. Even after years of teaching and studying this, I still sometimes wake up at three in the morning and have to remind myself, "I have exactly the time I need."

Hustle is not all it's cracked up to be, and to be successful at anything, we have to embrace the focus. The tools in this book are here to help you break old habits and embrace Focus Culture.

SIDEBAR: Productivity vs. Focus

Resist the urge to measure the quality of your day by the quantity of your accomplishments.

Productivity and Focus are not the same thing. Productivity is the by-product of focus. Our productivity, or specifically what we can produce in a set amount of time, is variable and therefore difficult to measure. Sometimes tasks take longer than you expect, or you're stuck waiting on someone else before you can proceed.

It's like focusing on non-scale victories for health. You're more successful when you focus on actions in your control, like what you eat or how you move. If you prioritize focus, productivity will follow.

If you base your success on how much you produce, you might be disappointed by something that was actually out of your control. If you prioritize focus it will always lead to better results.

CHAPTER 1:
LET'S REJECT HUSTLE CULTURE

FOCUS ON THIS

- Hustle Culture tells us to do more, more, more.
- Focus Culture puts us back in charge of our time, our projects, our calendars and our lives.
- Focus Culture is not about being more productive; it's about being more focused… there's a difference.

CHAPTER 2:

YOU WERE MEANT TO MAKE AN IMPACT

For over a decade I've worked with entrepreneurs just like you, so I know some of your strengths. You are really good at what you do and you were meant to make an impact. In fact, I know you are already making an impact. You have lots of brilliant ideas, too many to implement at once. You also take on multiple roles in business and in life. You most likely have many responsibilities, from taking care of children or other family members to managing a household and a variety of schedules. And this comes with a heavy mental load.

The truth is that while you know you are meant to make an impact, those other responsibilities make it hard to feel like you are making any progress towards your goals without working a million hours, getting overwhelmed, letting someone down, or even burning out entirely.

There has to be a better way, right?

It's not about getting more done, it's about getting the right things done.

Focus on Purpose and Impact

What is most important in the life you are building? It's easy to get caught up in the things that we should do, but if they aren't moving you towards your goals, you aren't focusing on the right things. Let's start there.

That most important thing? That is the "why" driving you. That's your purpose. Your purpose is the foundation of your business, and it rarely changes because it is rooted in your values as a person. These values help shape the big picture you want for your business and those you serve. It is the compass that keeps you moving forward in a specific direction, even if your path changes.

If you look back, there has probably been a common thread of what has been important to you throughout your life. You can probably connect the dots between all the different things you've done with this thread. This is your purpose.

Your impact is the tangible change you want to make in the world. It is rooted in your purpose. Impact is your vision for the near future, say the next year to 18 months. Your impact answers the question, "Where do we want to go?" There may be different ways to create this impact, but the impact you want to make doesn't change.

Perhaps the impact you want to make this year is to empower female real estate agents to sell more effectively. You might do this through a one-on-one mentoring program with new agents, or by speaking at conferences on the topic. Different paths, same impact. (And your impact might evolve each year or when you realize the impact you want to make.)

> "*Women have the power to make a change, to create a better world. Let us not squander this opportunity, but rise to the challenge and make an impact.*"
> —Malala Yousafzai

Before we go any further, I want you to stop and ask yourself what impact you want to make. We'll dive into this idea of impact throughout this book, but right now ask yourself:

What is the impact that I want to make for my clients, for my family, for my larger community, and, maybe most importantly, for myself?

This impact is going to act as a filter, a guiding light, the North Star for every other decision that you make as a business owner and person. This is your Most Important Work. The mindset of focus is about putting your Most Important Work in the time you have the most focus, so you need to be clear on your impact.

In the space provided on the following pages (or in your printable *Focused Workbook* available at http://focus-sessions.com/bookbonus), write down how you want to impact yourself, your family, your clients, your community, and the world. Then, based on what you said, write a one-line impact statement.

What is the impact that I want to make for...

My Clients:

My Family:

My Community:

Myself:

The World:

My Impact Statement:

Fill out one of the sentences below, Mad-Libs style...

I want to help ________________________________ become ______________________________ this year.

I want to show ______________________________ that they can ________________________ without ________________ ____________________.

I help ______________________________________ so they can ______________________________________.

I want ______________________________________ to know that they can ____________________________.

I support ______________________________________ to get _________________________________ so they can ________ __________________________.

Or write your own:

Find Your Highest Contribution

In his book *The Big Leap*, Gay Hendricks coined the term "Zone of Genius" to describe an individual's sweet spot of unique abilities, passions, and talents that bring them joy and fulfillment. Instead of trying to improve your weaknesses, focus on developing your strengths. Hendricks says when you're in your Zone of Genius, you'll feel more creative, productive, and make a bigger impact.

After years of sharing this message of your Zone of Genius, I've put my own spin on it, which I call Your Highest Contribution.

Your Highest Contribution is made of three parts:

1. your skill set (that's your Zone of Genius, the thing you are really good at)
2. the thing that people need, or the problem that only you can solve
3. your excitement level

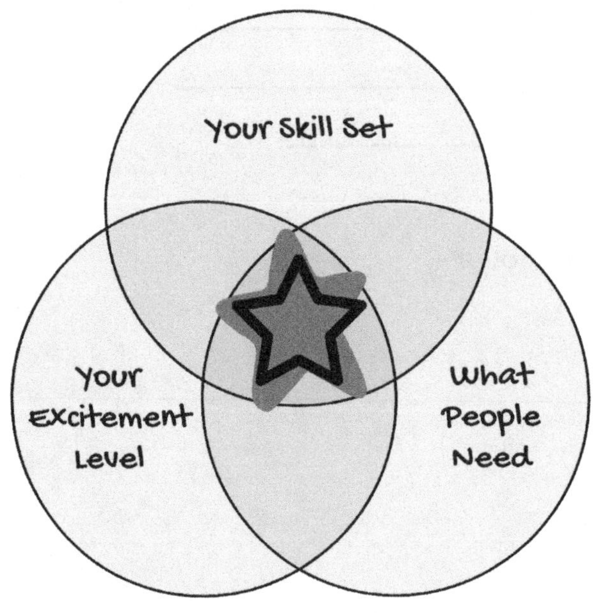

Your Highest Contribution is the special sauce that makes your businesses unique, and the thing that sets you apart from the others who do what you do. Most important, it's what lights you up and motivates you to run your business in the first place. If you have a skill around solving a problem, you can be an expert in your field, but when you add in your own excitement for that thing: THAT is your Highest Contribution.

My Zone of Genius is simplifying businesses and helping people break their goals into manageable tasks. But my Highest Contribution is changing what people believe about themselves when it comes to productivity and "getting stuff done." That mindset shift lights me up and creates an impact that will far outlast any project breakdown or launch plan.

The Business of Focus: Rachael Cook on Showing Up as a CEO

Racheal Cook is the host of the Promote Yourself to CEO podcast and founder of The CEO Collective, where they help women entrepreneurs sustainably scale their businesses without the hustle and burnout.

Early in her entrepreneurial journey, Racheal asked this question that changed the game for her business: "Am I truly showing up like the CEO of my business, not just in name, but in action?"

Here are some things Racheal considers when prioritizing her tasks, "If you are getting paid a thousand dollars an hour in your business, what would you do differently? How would you show up differently? What kinds of tasks would be on your plate each and every day? If you were getting paid a thousand dollars an hour from your business, would you be in your inbox? Would you be posting on social media? Would you be dealing with invoices and bookkeeping? Would you be tweaking behind the scenes in your website? Chances are you wouldn't, because you know that if you were getting paid at this level in your business, if your business were this successful, you would be out of the weeds. You would be out of the busy work."

She stresses that we cannot treat our time as an unlimited resource. Our time is the most precious resource we have, and we must invest it wisely. She uses this concept with her clients in what she calls the CEO Scorecard. Not all tasks are created equal, so Racheal divides up the tasks needed to run a business into:

- $10 an hour (admin level tasks)
- $100 an hour (higher level work like copywriting or client work)
- $1,000 an hour (growth-minded work like planning and skill building)
- $10,000 an hour (money-driven work like attraction-style marketing, sales)

She suggests tracking your time over the course of a week, like time tracking to bill a client at these different rates, and assigning a monetary value. Add up where you spent your time and use that as a guide for where you need to be devoting your attention and resources. The goal is to increase your CEO Score and also pay attention when you are spending too much time on the lower score tasks signaling you are not showing up like a CEO for your business.

Once you have this data, you can make choices to automate, delegate or decrease the time you spend on $10 an hour tasks and focus on the CEO tasks at the $1,000 and $10,000 point.

Learn more:
http://rachealcook.com
http://theceocollective.com

Do Less Better

Now that you know your desired impact, and you know your Highest Contribution, how do you find the time to do it?

I know, you're already adding to your mental to-do list, but the answer is not doing more. The answer is to Do Less Better.

Do Less Better means focusing on fewer goals and projects, and doing each of them to the best of your ability. (Note to all the perfectionists out there: Doing things to the best of your ability doesn't mean it needs to be perfect. I'm a fan of getting version 1.0 out there and improving as you go. Doing things to the best of your ability means that you are putting more energy and focus on fewer things so you can actually do those things solidly.)

Instead of spreading yourself too thin by trying to add in one more project or product, you choose your tasks strategically. By focusing on fewer high-impact tasks, you can achieve more meaningful results. By doing less, and doing it better, you can work smarter, not harder, and ultimately find more satisfaction in your work, not just relief that it's done. End result: Greater productivity and satisfaction, less overwhelm and burnout.

"Do Less Better" doesn't mean you'll never have a busy day or a tight deadline. Do Less Better is a mindset that you are doing enough. Later chapters will explain how to break things down, how to prioritize, where to get more realistic, and how to focus on the important things that push you forward. Remember, Focus Culture is all about being intentional instead of letting Hustle Culture burn you out.

CHAPTER 2:
YOU WERE MEANT TO MAKE AN IMPACT

FOCUS ON THIS

- The impact you want to make serves as your guiding principle and filter for your actions.
- Your Highest Contribution is that special sauce that only you can do, that lights you up and motivates you to move forward.
- "Do less better" is about working smarter and more intentionally, not just harder.

CHAPTER 3:

BUILD THE HOUSE YOU WANT TO LIVE IN

A few years ago, a close friend and I were talking about the intersections of our businesses and lives as we planned for the new year. She said a simple statement that had such a profound impact on me that I have repeated it a hundred times to myself and my clients.

> *"I want to make sure I'm building a house I want to live in."*

Whoa.

Sometimes, as we are building our businesses, it's easy to get mired in completing tasks and making lists that you forget to ask, "Where am I?" or "Where am I going?" or maybe most importantly, "Do I still want to head in this direction?"

The first place to start (or revisit) when you are thinking about how you are spending your time is to (re)define the house you want to live in.

It's like planning a road trip: We need to know our destination. We might not know the exact route or all the stops along the way, but knowing our end destination makes all the planning possible. Knowing where we're headed also acts as a filter for all the things we should pack or do along the way. Should we pack our ski parka for a trip to Florida? Probably not, nor do we need our snorkeling gear for a trip to Kansas.

When we are not clear on our destination, we can bog ourselves down with unnecessary items. "Maybe I should buy this webinar course" or "I better join this program in case I want to teach this topic one day" or "I should dance on TikTok, because someone else is doing it successfully" or "I have to go to this networking event, in case someone there wants to hire me."

Without knowing where we are heading, we can get caught doing a lot of "shoulds." When we know our destination, we can make decisions that get us there more efficiently. We spend our time, money, and energy building a house we want to live in.

Our road trip destination is our overall purpose, tied to our desired impact. It can act as a filter to make sure we are building the house we want to live in.

Ideal Future State

Your life is so much bigger than your business. While your business's desired impact might be a very important part of the house you want to live in, step back and look at your whole life and ask: "What is the house I want to live in?"

To answer these questions, I suggest the Ideal Future State exercise. This is a visioning exercise that transports you from where you are now to a spot in the future, 3, 5 or even 10 years out — whatever feels like the right amount of time to look into the future.

Give yourself some time and space for this exercise. Close your door and sit comfortably. Close your eyes and take a few deep breaths. Picture yourself in a specific spot at that specific moment in the future.

Look around in your mind's eye: What do you see? Where are you? Who is with you? What are you doing in this space in time? Don't take any notes yet; simply look around your "space" and notice what is included in this ideal future state.

Below are a few more prompts to think about while you vision this spot in the future:

- Where are you?
- Where are you living?
- What does the room you are in look like?
- Who is with you? In the room, in your house, in your life...?
- What have you received accolades for?
- How are you making money?
- How much are you making?
- Who are your clients?
- What problem are you solving?
- Who are you working with as your team or collaborators?
- What are you selling?
- Where do you work?
- What does your workspace look like?
- When do you work each week?
- What months do you work?
- What are your work hours?
- What does time off look like?
- How does your day start?
- What do you do at the end of the work day?
- How do you feel at the end of the day?

*If you'd like to listen to an audio prompt of this exercise, head to http://focus-sessions.com/bookbonus for a downloadable audio file.

Once you are done with the visualization, open your eyes, let the images sink in, and then take some time to journal what you remember.

Don't try to answer every question. Instead, notice: What were the big ideas and themes that came up? What stuck with you?

Jot down your "ahas" and realizations below, or in your *Focused Workbook*.

General Thoughts:

Then think about what came up: Did anything surprise you? How different was your Ideal Future State from where you are today? What was the same?

Look back through your thoughts, and take notice of...

Values or Overarching Themes:

Anything Surprising or Unexpected:

Going through this exercise is a great way to start to craft the image and the plan for the house you want to live in. This is the first step in knowing where you are headed and what you want to focus on.

Find Your Flow

Work-life balance is a myth. There, I said it.

Balance is hard to achieve; one little tip of the scale can throw everything out of whack. Also, the term "work-life" implies that there are only two binary states: there is work, and there is everything else — and that somehow those two things are supposed to balance out. That sounds like an awful lot of things to cram into the "life" side of the scale.

I actually think the whole thing is "life."

Life is made up of many different pieces, and work is just one of them. It's not about balance; it's about flow. It's about moving between all the different pieces of our life — work, relationships, health, personal development, hobbies, and everything else — and pouring attention where it's needed, then flowing to another section to do the same. (In Chapter 17, we'll talk about my spinning plates analogy, which applies perfectly here as well.)

One tool to help visualize all these areas is called **The Wheel of Life.** The Wheel of Life is a pie chart with a wedge for each of the different areas in your life. Your chart can have whatever areas are important to you, but here is a suggestion:

- Health
- Personal Development
- Spirituality
- Hobbies
- Finances
- Friends
- Business/Work
- Relationships

You need time for all of these areas and you might even have other categories you want to include or swap out to personalize this to your life. (But you'll notice your business is only one slice of the pie ... ahem.)

Step One: Rank how you are feeling about each area on a scale of 1–10, and shade them in on the wheel. An 8 or 9 means it is flowing really well — you've been able to give that area some attention, and it's feeling pretty good. A 2 or 3 doesn't mean you are bad or out of balance. It serves as an indication that it is time to flow some energy and attention into that area.

Here's a couple of samples of what your wheel might look like!

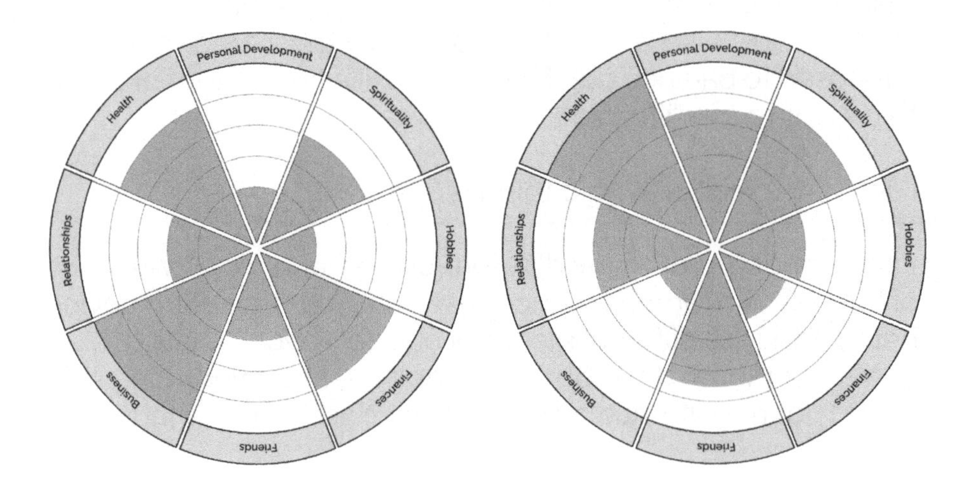

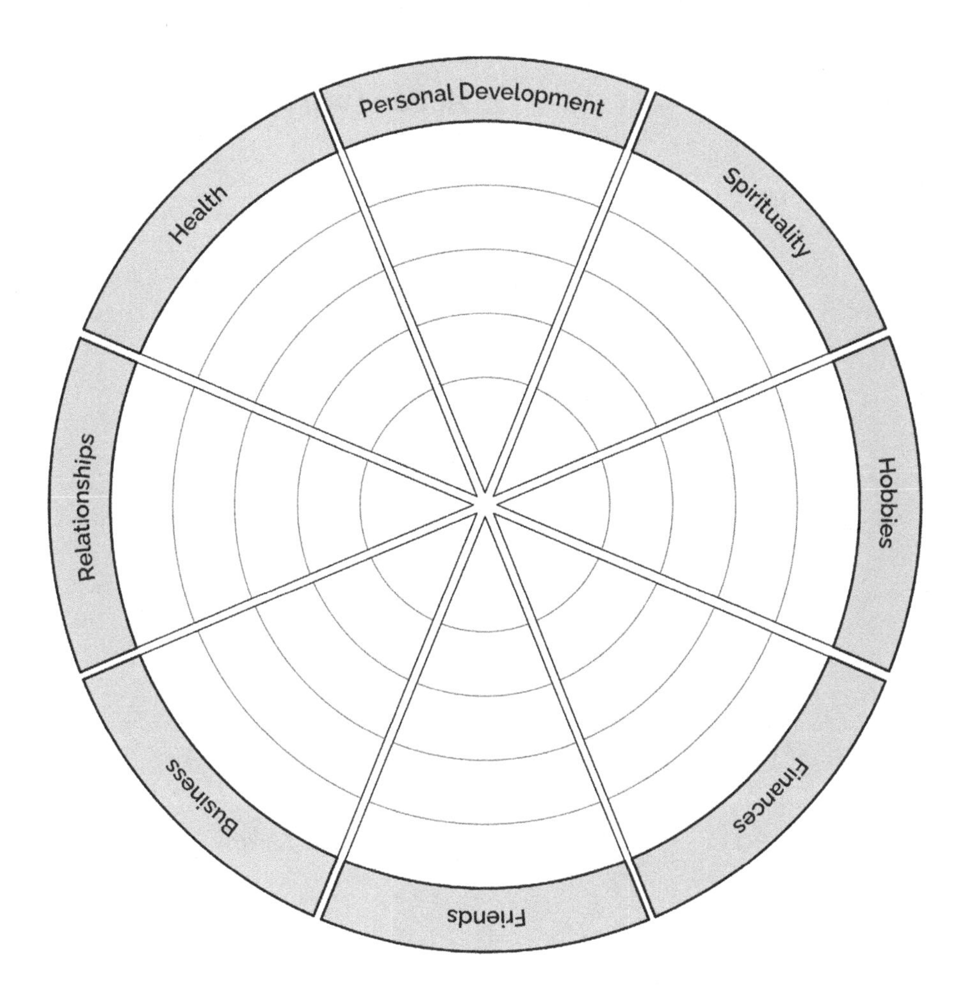

Step Two: Pick 1–3 sections that could use some attention for the next 90 days (or any amount of time you choose). You don't have to focus on all the areas all the time! That's a Hustle Culture mindset. Remember we're trying to embrace Focus Culture.

Step Three: For each of those sections, choose 1–3 things that would help raise it one number. Notice I didn't say move that section up to a 10. Just focus on improving by one. If your personal development is feeling like a 2, what is one thing you could do to make it feel like a 3? That is a lot more doable, and a lot less pressure, than trying to jump from a 2 to a 10!

Focus Area: *Action I will take:*

Focus Area: *Action I will take:*

Focus Area: *Action I will take:*

Revisit this Wheel of Life regularly to track your progress. Quarterly is a great goal, but choose another time period if it works better for you. You can pick a new area to focus on for the next 90 days, or pick the same areas and choose another way to move up one more number.

There is a blank wheel in your *Focused Workbook* so you can print a clean copy any time you need it (find your workbook at http://focus-sessions.com/bookbonus).

What's Working and What's Not

Now that we have our destination, we can start to think about our route. Using the assessment of our whole wheel, we can determine what is working and what needs to change.

Change is a process, not an event. Think about the process of making your life more enjoyable, impactful, and focused. It's not about fixing something broken; it's about making meaningful, consistent progress towards the way you would like to feel and away from what is not serving you. Remember, progress isn't always linear:

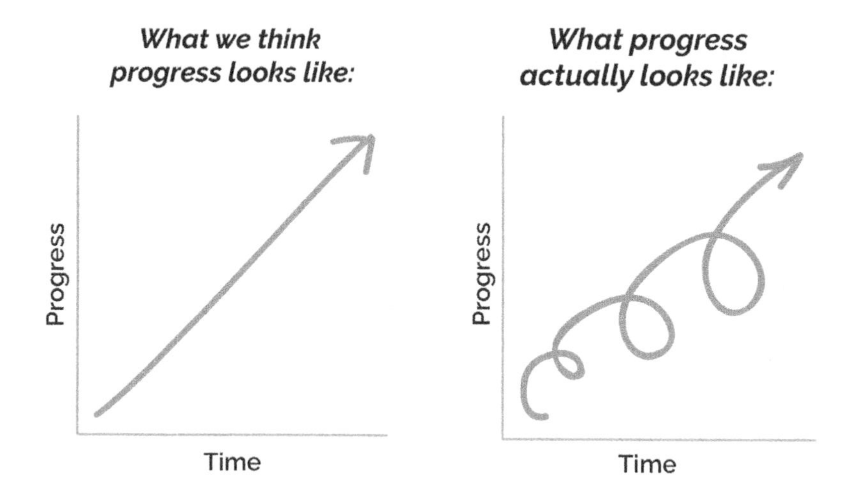

To make meaningful progress towards change, you must know what is currently working and what is not.

Let's make a list. (I love lists!) Make a line down the center of your paper (or use the page included in your *Focused Workbook*).

On one side, write what is working well in your life or in your business. On the other side, write what feels a little bumpy or not working quite the way you want.

Even though it might seem easier to focus on the "what's not working" side, the "what is working" side is as important. It's human nature to dismiss or ignore what's working, instead of taking something good and making it great. You know what they say: The way you do one thing is the way you do everything. It's important to acknowledge what's working to learn from it and apply this "recipe for success" to the things that are not working as well.

What's Working:	***What's NOT Working:***

Your Recipe for Success

You already know how to succeed. You do. No matter how you feel about your current situation, you have succeeded a million times in the past. And if you have done something before, you can do it again. "But Megan," you're thinking, "I've never done THIS thing before. I don't know how to succeed at this new thing I'm doing."

You do, because you have a Recipe for Success.

Think about it. If you have made chocolate chip cookies before, you know how to follow a recipe and you also know that you like to add a few extra chocolate chips and cook the cookies for a little less time than the recipe says because you like them chewy. So when it comes time to try a brand new cookie recipe, you already know what to do, even if you've never made THAT exact cookie.

Let's make another list! (I told you I love lists.)

List 25 accomplishments you are proud of from the past year.

They can be big or little. They can be business or family or personal. Just don't stop until you get 25. Think about all the things you have done recently that you deemed successes. Perhaps it was dealing with a difficult conversation well, or launching a program, or writing a well-received blog post. Write that down. Pick one of your wins or accomplishments or successes ... whatever you want to call it. How did you do it? WHY were you successful? What did you do to make that project or task work?

Maybe you prepared ahead of time for the difficult conversation, spent time listening to the other's concerns, and spoke your own truth. Maybe you kept your program launch simple and planned what would be included ahead of time. Maybe you wrote that blog post from your heart about a topic you knew others had been struggling with as well. Once you know why something was successful, you have a recipe for future successes.

My Wins: *Why?:*

1.
2.
3.
4.
5.
6.
7.
8.
9.
10.
11.
12.
13.
14.
15.
16.
17.
18.
19.
20.
21.
22.
23.
24.
25.

Go back to each of your 25 wins and write why it was successful. What did you do in order to accomplish that?

Look for themes. What are the three things you usually do that result in success? That is your Recipe for Success.

Your Ideal Future State, your Wheel of Life, and your Recipe for Success are tools to discover the guiding principles for what you want to focus on in your life.

FOCUS AFFIRMATION

Start WHERE YOU ARE

CHAPTER 3:
BUILD THE HOUSE YOU WANT TO LIVE IN

FOCUS ON THIS

- Your Ideal Future State helps you visualize the "house you want to live in." By focusing on your vision for the future, you can be more clear on the actions you want to take today.
- Your life is made up of many different areas, and you won't rank all of them a 10 all the time. Pick one or two areas at a time to focus on in your Wheel of Life to increase your satisfaction in that area by just one number.
- You have already had past successes; use those to inform how to create future ones by identifying your Recipe for Success!

CHAPTER 4:

WHY YOU CAN'T FOCUS – AND WHY YOU NEED TO

By this point you're probably getting excited about what your life could look like with clarity about the future you've envisioned and the impact you want to make. You're even starting to see how you can replicate what's worked before with your Recipe for Success. But you might also be feeling overwhelmed wondering how you'll get from where you are now to where you want to be.

The answer is focus.

Why You Need Focus

This whole book is an ode to why focus is important. One you may not hear often is this: **Focus is actually self-care.**

I bet you've heard some version of "make time for self-care" in every article you've ever read on work-life balance, burnout, or even productivity. But what if focus IS the self-care you need?

How many times do you find yourself texting your partner about dinner plans, messaging another parent about kid pick up, responding to a client email, letting the dog out, reminding yourself you really need to get toilet paper, and trying to log onto Zoom for a client call ... all at the same time?

I'm exhausted just thinking about it, and also ... it's not that unusual.

What if instead of trying to do all the things at the same time, you focused on ONE thing?

When I said that, I bet either your shoulders dropped and you exhaled a little ... or you panicked about getting things done. Let's talk about how focus works so you can get a little breathing room.

It's draining to multitask, and even if we think we are good at it, research shows that we're not. We know that the brain cannot concentrate on two or more tasks simultaneously. Instead, it rapidly switches between tasks, a process called task-switching, which can lead to decreased productivity and increased errors. Additionally, multitasking can lead to cognitive fatigue, making it harder to retain information. Studies have also found that multitasking can negatively impact learning and memory. Overall, research suggests that it is more efficient to focus on one task at a time, rather than trying to multitask.

You've probably experienced this. You spend all day trying to get an email out or write a landing page, because you're distracted responding to things that seem to need your urgent attention. You've probably also been stunned how quickly you can get a similar task done when you turn off the distractions to have time and space to focus.

Focus is less draining than multitasking, and it can even be energizing. Getting into a state where your work and effort seems to flow feels amazing — and we feel good about ourselves when we make progress (instead of moving the same things from one to-do list to the next).

Focus is a gift to your future self. When you focus now, you are actually less stressed and exhausted, which can make you feel calmer and happier later. People tell us they sleep better after attending one of our Focus Sessions virtual coworking events, and that their ability to focus improves overall when they attend multiple sessions to continue practicing their focus.

When you focus and finish a project quickly – instead of multi-tasking across multiple tasks – you have time for other things you want to do later. You accomplish more during your focus time, allowing you to move on to other important things in your day and in your life.

Why You Can't Focus

Our brains are constantly bombarded with distractions in our modern environment, pings and dings from our phones and social media, emails, and the constant stimulation of the Internet. Additionally, our brains have evolved to constantly seek out new information, which can make it difficult to focus on a single task for an extended period of time. We have so much access to information there is always something more to learn, do, or respond too. Our brains are working overtime on how to process all the information we are constantly being fed. Furthermore, some people may have conditions that impact their attention, such as ADHD, which make it even harder for them to focus. Other factors that contribute to a lack of focus include stress, lack of sleep, and an overstimulated mind.

A global pandemic, social unrest, and natural disasters have all exacerbated these focus-crushing factors. The pandemic has had a long term impact on our brains in ways the mental health industry is just beginning to understand.

The pandemic had another effect, for better or for worse: it forced us to stop doing everything. When we were able to start doing things again, many of us asked ourselves if we still wanted the lifestyle we had before. Whether it was specifically what we were doing for work, or the way we approached work, the reentry made us question how we had always done things. That left a lack of clarity and certainty, two things that make focus hard to come by.

Even if we are really clear on what we want to do, there is so much to pull away our attention. Each time we are distracted, it can take 6–23 minutes to refocus on our task. We're not only distracted by that ping from our phone or the ding on our computer; we're distracted by the inside of our own brains as well. Anxiety and stress are at an all time high, so it's no wonder if you get preoccupied by that voice inside your head.

When people share what they struggle with when it comes to focus, the answers usually fit into three categories:

I don't know what to focus on.

I don't have time to focus.

I don't know how to focus.

Does one of these resonate for you? Maybe more than one? We are going to spend the rest of this book addressing all three.

Focus in Action: John Robinson

Before Focus Sessions, I didn't have as regular a schedule for dedicated work. I had a lot to accomplish and found it challenging to get enough done.

I think the biggest lesson was the dedication of time to focus and take care of my most important projects. I now have Focus Sessions blocked out on my calendar. Even if I don't make it, the time is set aside and only gets replaced with careful consideration. The time for me is the priority, where before it wasn't as predictable or solid.

The biggest transformation is how it feels easier to get into a space of focus, and deeper at that. Working with the Focus Sessions community has transformed me so that my practice is better, in and out of the sessions.

I have more peace, because I'm getting more of the most important things done, and I feel good because I'm taking care of myself and blocking out the time for myself.

You can learn more about Coach John at: http://CoachJohn.help

FOCUS AFFIRMATION

FOCUS is Self Care

CHAPTER 4:
WHY YOU CAN'T FOCUS — AND WHY YOU NEED TO

FOCUS ON THIS

- Focus is a form of self-care. Your future will benefit from the focus you put in now.
- Focus is hard, especially in the digital age: your environment, your surroundings and your own brain can make focus a challenge.
- Many people struggle with focus. They usually say, "I don't know how to focus," "I don't have the time to focus," or "I don't know what to focus on."

PART II

IS YOUR TO-DO LIST SABOTAGING YOUR PRODUCTIVITY? — WHAT TO FOCUS ON

“Perfectionism is not the same thing as striving to be our best. Perfectionism is the belief that if we live perfect, look perfect, and act perfect, we can minimize or avoid the pain of blame, judgment, and shame.”

Brené Brown

CHAPTER 5:

THE ART OF A WELL-CRAFTED TO-DO LIST

I love a to-do list. Digital, on paper, with a bold black marker or color-coded text, I love them all. When it comes to getting things done, you likely also turn to your trusted to-do list. It's the perfect tool for focus, right? Or is it?

If your to-do list contains everything from "launch a podcast" to "pay a phone bill," "sign a kid up for baseball," and "redo website homepage"... your to-do list might actually be sabotaging your productivity. So let's start with what should be on your to-do list—and what shouldn't—and where those other items should go.

When I ask a room of entrepreneurs to tell me their goals for this quarter or this year, people shout out things like "new website," "launch a product," and "get a speaking gig!" But then I ask, "What is on your to-do list?" People tell me "new website," "launch a product," and "get a speaking gig!"

The problem is that these things aren't actually goals OR to-do list tasks. They are actually projects. When you misname them as line items you can check off a list, even in your mind, it leads to a feeling of overwhelm. You think you aren't making progress, or you're bad at time management, or you aren't good at focusing, or whatever your inner critic tells you is why you aren't moving forward.

Let's pull all the way back and look at my Nimble Planning System:

Purpose	Value	WHY we are here	Lifetime
Impact	Vision	WHERE we want to go	Year +
Goals	Priorities	HOW we'll do it	Quarter
Projects	Milestones	WHAT we're going to do	Monthly
Tasks	Intention	WHEN we will take action	Daily

Remember in Chapter 2 when you read about Purpose and Impact? Your Purpose and Impact serve as a compass, a guiding light, always pointing to your true north no matter the course you take. Let's review those concepts and see how goals, projects, and tasks flow out of them, because understanding how they all work together is how you define your Most Important Work.

Purpose

Your business's Purpose is rooted in your values as a person by answering the question, "Why are we here?" Your Purpose is the foundation of your business, and it rarely shifts. Your Purpose is the compass that keeps you moving forward, even if your path changes.

Impact

Impact answers the question, "Where do we want to go?" This is the tangible change you want to see in the world.

Annual revenue goals are part of your Impact Planning. How much money do you want to bring in? How much will you pay yourself? How much will you reinvest in your business and your community? All of these can be achieved in different ways, but the Impact and the money you want to make stays constant.

Goals

Goals answer the question, "How are we going to make the impact?" These line up with your quarterly priorities. Each 90 days you ask yourself, "What is my priority, this quarter, to make the Impact I want to make this year?"

Quarterly goals might shift or morph based on big picture things. Maybe one quarter you want to be able to take time off or you need to focus on caring for a family member. You can adjust your goals to fit those needs, while still driving towards your impact.

Maybe you focus on selling a DIY product during times when your children need more support with school, but focus on a one-on-one offer at a point in the year when your clients need more hands-on support.

Goals don't belong on your to-do list. Goals are the big picture. A goal might be to "reach a larger audience with my message," or "help my clients learn that they can approach their nutrition intuitively."

I believe that goals should be inspirational. They belong somewhere visible, like your whiteboard or a Post-it on your mirror, to motivate you to keep going and pull you back to the Impact you want to have.

Projects

Projects are "What we are going to do?" Think of projects as the milestones or pieces on the way to the goal. If your goal is to reach a larger audience, a project could be starting a podcast. If your goal is to help clients learn about intuitive nutrition, a project could be launching a new offer based on your methodology. Notice that you could reach the same goal with other projects. Instead of starting a podcast, you could reach a larger audience by speaking at summits or on other people's podcasts. The project is the way you have chosen to achieve your goal.

While goals belong on your mirror to inspire you, projects belong in a project management system, broken down into smaller steps, which may eventually move onto your to-do- list. This could be a tool like Asana, ClickUp, a Google spreadsheet, or simply a page in your notebook where all the steps of your project live. Projects do not go on your daily to-do list.

Tasks

Tasks are all the individual steps that make up a project. Tasks are what go on the to-do list. If your goal is "grow a larger audience," your project could be, "launch a podcast," then the tasks would be the smaller steps, like "research equipment," "order microphone," "brainstorm guests," and "write landing page."

Tasks should be single-step items that can go from not done, to done in one step. I'll talk more about moving from project to task in the next chapter.

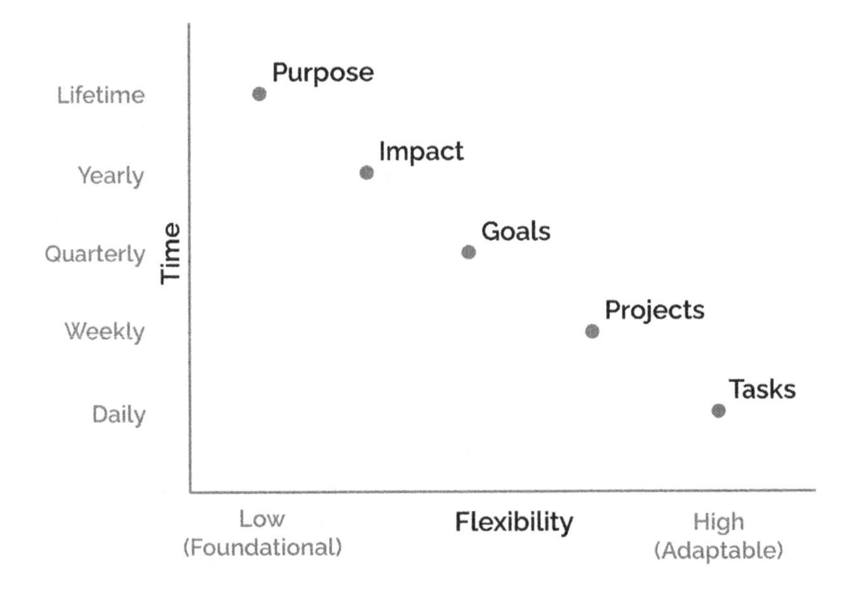

Together, these make up the Nimble Planning System, which sets a solid foundation and allows for high flexibility. If you've spent a lot of time pivoting, you might wonder if planning is actually worth it. It is, and that's the beauty of a Nimble Plan. This planning process lets you stay rooted in what is fundamental in your business and be agile enough to pivot as the economy, your energy, your family needs, and client demands change.

Understanding the different parts of the Nimble Planning System also helps you make the most of your to-do list and keep your Most Important Work at the forefront.

Focus In Action: Katie Bratland

I have always been a bit reactionary with my work day and usually would just jump into whatever was most urgent without taking stock of everything I needed to do. Since starting with Focus Sessions Planning, I am so much more confident that I am working on the right things. Now instead of feeling overwhelmed, I have a system in place to help me plan my day, my week, and my projects.

I have learned how to plan more effectively, specifically putting tasks on my list, not projects. Wow! That was such a revelation to me. It seems so obvious, but that "little" piece of direction was transformational. Also, breaking everything down into the smallest task possible so that we can more easily see what it takes to complete a project. So, so good!

Because of Focus Sessions, I have been able to stay on top of what needs to get done and more importantly, figure out my biggest priority each week and each day. I used to jump from task to task instead of thinking through everything I needed to get done, but now I think through and decide when to accomplish each thing.

SIDEBAR: Focus Buckets

You've probably heard the acronym SMART when it comes to goal setting. It stands for making sure your goals are Specific, Measurable, Attainable, Relevant, and Time-bound. I actually don't believe your goals need to be smart; I believe they need to be inspirational. Your goals need to motivate you to do the work it's going to take to accomplish them. If your goals aren't giving you the chills when you say them out loud, it's going to be harder to find the motivation to complete them. Save the smart details for the project level.

Now that you know the difference between a goal, a project, and a task, you can choose only tasks for your focus time. Instead of sitting down to "work on book," you can "edit chapter 1" or "approve design."

Having a clear task is important for focus, and those tasks fall into three buckets.

- Visioning & Planning
- Deep Work
- Clearing the Deck

We'll look at each bucket in depth in the upcoming chapters.

CHAPTER 5:
THE ART OF A WELL-CRAFTED TO-DO LIST

FOCUS ON THIS

- The first step in knowing what to focus on is identifying the difference between goals, projects, and tasks.
- The Nimble Planning System takes you from your purpose, which is a big overarching way of living, all the way down to the individual tasks on your daily to-do list.
- Projects are the milestones that get you to your larger goals and the impact you want to make. Tasks are the individual units of work that go on your to-do list.

CHAPTER 6:

THE IMPORTANCE OF VISIONING AND PLANNING

As CEO of your business and life, your number one job (no matter what your Highest Contribution is) is to be the visionary of your company. While it's great to get support, input and coaching, at the end of the day, only you can drive the vision of your company.

The same is true for your family and your life. You are ultimately the only one who can envision the exact path you want your future to take. Since this level of big thinking is the single most important role, then you'd better set aside time to do it!

Start with Your Vision, Create a Plan

Schedule some time to think big. This kind of visioning work comes before you set any goals or choose projects. If you haven't done this in a while, set aside time for visioning—turn off notifications, put on Do Not Disturb Mode, clear your head, and settle into thinking mode. Think about the exercises you did in Part 1 about the house you want to live in, and your Ideal

Future State. This might be time to journal, take a walk, do a guided meditation, or take a shower. Don't force this process. Let your vision marinate.

Your vision is what will drive your plan. Planning is how we'll bring this vision to life.

Planning saves valuable time. It is said that one hour spent planning can save 10 hours on execution. Plus, spending time planning out how you are going to get to that vision can save hours of frustrations when you hit a deadend or a roadblock you didn't anticipate.

SIDEBAR: 90 Day Plans

While it might be traditional to set yearly goals and plans, it has been proven that shorter time frames, specifically 90 days, is a more effective way to accomplish your goals. Ninety days, or a quarter, is long enough to put a plan in place and see it through to the results, but it is short enough to keep your eye on the finish line the whole time. Especially for small business owners, quarterly planning allows you to be agile and make shifts as other parts of your business and life shift. Ninety days is also a great milestone for marking progress. Setting aside time each quarter to review your accomplishments and plan your projects for the next quarter is a proven way to build momentum in your business and life.

Turning your vision into a plan is something I teach my clients to do quarterly. We think about the impact we want to make.

We set our goals. We choose our projects. **This is part of our 90-Day Plan.**

Then we break our projects down into tasks and timelines. **That's project planning.**

Then each week we **plan our week** to make sure we prioritize the tasks that complete the projects that reach our goals. (We'll talk about weekly planning in Chapter 12).

Plan Your Project

I once heard a parenting expert say that telling a young child to clean their room is really overwhelming to them, but if you help them break their cleaning into specific tasks, it's much easier. Telling them to start by picking up all the dirty laundry gives them a clear, specific task to complete, and they can see when that task is completed. Then you can move on to putting away all the books, then the stuffed animals, etc.

This is the exact method I use for getting projects done too. Instead of sitting down to "work," decide which tasks you are going to complete in a set amount of time. You'll have more wins and build momentum on your project.

So how do you know what the pieces of your project are? Plan it out. Go get your Post-it notes. These are the steps I take to plan every project.

1. Define "done"

Start by defining what "done" looks like for your project. Entrepreneurs are notorious for moving the goalposts on projects. If you choose a vague project like "new website," the project may never feel done. It's important to be specific and define the end product or where you'll stop. That could mean "home, about, and services pages live by the end of Q1."

Write down what "done" looks like on a Post-it note and stick it somewhere you'll see it often. This will help you stay focused and on track. Another great tool is to set smaller milestones within your project and create what "done" looks like for each of those milestones. Maybe you want to have all the content for your course organized in a Google Doc or update your homepage as a milestone for your website redesign project. Whatever your goal is, write it down on your Post-it note so you have a clear idea of what "done" means.

2. Identify tasks

Next break down your project into all the tasks needed to get to that version of done. To do that, write each task you think of on a separate Post-it note and stick it on your table or wall. Take at least 10 minutes to brainstorm as many tasks as possible. Don't edit yourself during this process, just write everything down that comes to mind. You can reject or combine tasks later.

When you think you've listed everything, notice if any of your tasks look like they might take more than an hour. Completing a task is most effective when it can be done in an hour or less (ideally in 15-25 minutes). If any of your Post-it notes look bigger than that, break that task down into smaller tasks. Remember: **A task is a single step — the smallest unit of work.**

3. Organize your to-dos

Once you've finished your brainstorm and broken things into individual tasks, organize the Post-its by priority or chronology. Next, sort tasks by what is a "must-do" and what would be a "nice-to-do" if you have time. I'm a big fan of getting things out into the world. You can always add more later in version 2.0. Once you've prioritized, put your tasks in order of what you need to do first, second, third, etc. You can also indicate which tasks you might be able to delegate or outsource (more on delegation later.)

4. Assign a time

Now make sure your ingredients will fit in your container. (You'll hear way more about my soup analogy, as we go!) Grab a red pen and write on each Post-it note how long you think each step will take, then add up all the time estimates. This will help you plan out how many hours this project will take.

Aim for your time estimates to add up to only 80% of your total available work hours because sometimes things go wrong or take longer than expected. If you have 12 hours to complete a project over two weeks, your estimates should only total 10 hours. This gives you the buffer time we'll discuss more in depth in Chapter 9.

Will your project fit in the time you have available? If not, you can adjust the deadline, remove some tasks/redefine what "done" looks like, or move other things to make more time available for this project (e.g., get more childcare, move another deadline).

5. Fit it into your week

When will you actually get things done? It's time to fit it into your week. Block off the time you have available for the project and start assigning tasks to those blocks. I usually join the Monday morning Focus Sessions to kick off my week with a planning session.

SIDEBAR: Sprints

Have a really big project? Consider breaking your project into two-week time containers called sprints. Creating a two-week sprint tells you where you're going to focus your attention for a finite amount of time and helps you build momentum to complete larger projects.

Begin creating your sprint by looking at the container you have. Look at your calendar for the next two weeks and think about how much time you can realistically devote to your project. Remember, this isn't all your available time — this is the time you can carve out for this project, without neglecting the day-to-day operations of your business. Make sure you take into consideration all the other things you need to do, like eating, taking care of your family, and having downtime. You can make strategic decisions to work outside of your normal work hours or get extra help if needed, but make sure to do it consciously.

Once you know how much time you have, pick a project that fits that container. Then break down all the tasks to get you to that milestone and schedule them. Remember to leave yourself a little buffer time on the project.

You can certainly plan back-to-back 2-week sprints, but I like to give myself a little time in between sprints. Dedicating a 2-week sprint to one project each month or quarter is a great way to make significant progress and build momentum.

Focus In Action: Tori Boats

While my work focuses on coaching high-achieving company founders, I was finding a need to put my own accountability systems in place. I had wanted to be consistent with CEO planning, but without accountability, I always skipped it. I just couldn't commit to the habit.

Guided Focus Sessions have given me a disciplined coworking experience and a dedicated time with accountability to do my planning – with guidance, so I wouldn't get distracted to boot.

I've learned how to actually plan a project. While I knew the steps, I couldn't get through the process. My mind got scattered, and I couldn't bring myself to make a game plan while staring at my giant list of tasks. It felt overwhelming and I would give up, not making a lick of progress. Having support to take you past overwhelm to create a plan is a huge benefit.

I have consistently shown up for myself to work ON the business every week since joining! I haven't missed once. I joined in on several other coworking sessions to get Planning, Deep Work, and Clearing the Deck work done, too!

I feel more in control of where my business is headed, confident that I can execute on my shoot-for-the-moon projects, and a sense of pride at all that I've accomplished.

See more about Tori and her coaching businesses: http://toriboats.com

FOCUS AFFIRMATION

Planning PAYS OFF

CHAPTER 6:
THE IMPORTANCE OF VISIONING AND PLANNING

FOCUS ON THIS

- Your number-one job as the CEO of your business (and life) is to be the visionary. Set aside dedicated as well as unstructured time to do so.
- Planning your projects before you start working on them will save you time and frustration and allow you to be more intentional with your work.
- Breaking big projects into 2-week sprints is a great way to build momentum to get bigger projects completed.

CHAPTER 7:

MAKE TIME FOR DEEP WORK AND PRIORITIZE YOUR HIGHEST CONTRIBUTION

You've created a vision, planned out your project, and broken that project down into tasks. Now it's time to do some "Deep Work." Deep Work tasks require periods of concentration or uninterrupted thought, and if you devote the right energy to them, you can get into a "flow state."

The concept of Deep Work was coined by author Cal Newport, a computer science professor, author, and speaker known for his books on the intersection of technology and work. Newport says that the state of flow found when focusing on Deep Work allows individuals to produce better results in less time.

Think about the last time you tried to write a proposal or figure out why something wasn't working. You might have spent several frustrating hours or days on it while you field calls from clients, respond to team members on Slack, get sidetracked on social media, and wonder if you need groceries for dinner. Then you had 45 uninterrupted minutes to actually focus, and you got it done.

That's the power of focus for Deep Work.

Deep Work could look like writing a sales page, creating course content, editing a chapter in your novel, writing a proposal, drafting your TED talk, doing a lesson for a class, or prepping for taxes. Deep Work is sometimes a simple task that needs your full attention, but it often overlaps with your most important work or your Highest Contribution, the things that move your business and your big dreams forward. You should spend the bulk of your prime focus time on Deep Work.

Eyes on the Prize — Will It Make the Boat Go Faster?

Think back to the impact you said you wanted to make in Chapter 2. Remember I said that this impact is going to act as a filter, a guiding light, a north star for every other decision that you make? People often forget to use that filter. You get sidetracked by work you're good at or that brings in revenue, even if it doesn't move you toward your goals or the impact you want to make.

In 1998, the British rowing team set a goal of winning a gold medal at the Sydney Olympics in 2000. It was a big goal for a mediocre team. But guess what? They did it! After their win, the coach wrote a book called Will It Make the Boat Go Faster about strategies the team used to succeed. The team used that title question to evaluate and prioritize all their actions and decisions. If the answer was "yes," then they would proceed. If the answer was "no," then they avoided the activity or did not go forward with that action.

I love this concept for making day-to-day decisions around your Highest Contribution and the impact you want to make. If my current goal is to help 1000 people find their focus to make the impact they are meant to make, I can use a similar question to assure that every action taken is directly related to having that impact or achieving that goal.

For example, if my goal question is, "Will this get me to 1000 members?" and then someone wants to hire me to help them create a marketing campaign for their business, I can ask myself, "Will taking on this work get me to 1000 members?" If the answer is no, I save that time to work toward my goal. If a team member needs me to review their work, I can use my "Will this ..." question to realize that if I spend all my time in Slack, I am not working towards my goal.

"But," I hear you saying, "I do need to review some work from my team." Yes, you still have to run the day-to-day operations of your business ... but you don't want your Deep Work tasks to get interrupted by smaller ones. Save these team check-ins for a Clearing the Deck time block, which we'll discuss in the next chapter.

Below (or in your *Focused Workbook*), create your own filter question to help you decide where to put your energy and attention.

My Filter Question:

SIDEBAR: Dealing with Distractions

What happens if somebody asks you to do something that doesn't move you toward your Impact? You may hesitate to turn down revenue, but you don't want to steal time from yourself. When faced with a decision like that, consider two things:

1. How does the revenue fit into your big picture? Is this an easy project that would help float you until your dream is generating revenue on its own?
2. Are you solely focused on money in the bank, or are you looking at the full profitability picture? (Keep reading to explore the three lenses of profitability).

Don't Get Distracted by the Little Stuff

You know you have to turn down some opportunities and steer clear of distractions if you want to keep moving toward your goals. Life sometimes throws a curveball that you need to adapt to, but if you keep waiting for things to settle down, you'll never get into your Deep Work. Most of the time, day-to-day distractions get in the way. If you're attempting to do Deep Work, you cannot allow yourself to multitask by responding to client requests or scheduling appointments, managing your team or going through your inbox, following up on that invoice or cleaning the mess on your desk.

Yes, all those things need to get done, but if you're not careful, they eat up the whole day. What if you scheduled time to complete those tasks? Instead of responding to a message or email when it arrives, you put it aside until the scheduled time? This approach is called Clearing the Deck. It's focus bucket three, and we'll cover it in the next chapter.

Focus In Action: Angie Hardison

During Focus to Finish — a 2-week productivity sprint offered by Focus Sessions — it was my goal to complete a personal website project I had been putting off for a while. At the end of the first week, during coaching, I realized there was no way I was going to be able to complete my project.

I was encouraged to set a smaller, more realistic goal — writing all the copy for the Home and About pages — so that I could complete something within the allotted time. It felt good to make progress on this task I had been procrastinating on, and I knew what the next steps would be to continue to work on the bigger project.

I worked on it for another 2 weeks and was able to complete the bigger goal I had initially set.

It felt great to complete my project! I felt encouraged and equipped to break down the project into smaller tasks that I could easily manage in an hour or two. This helped me chisel away at it and finally get it done.

Check out Angie and her business:
http://awakendesignsolutions.com

The Business of Focus: Leah Neaderthal on Profitability and Your Highest Contribution

Leah Neaderthal is the founder and CEO of Smart Gets Paid. She helps consultants get paid more for their work.

When you think of the word profitability, you probably think about money, but Leah uses the framework of the Profitability Triangle, which includes three lenses: financial, professional, and emotional. Leah cautions that only looking through the lens of financial profitability can lead to overwork and taking on work that is not ideal. When you reframe how you think about profitability, you can take on work that not only brings in money, but is personally fulfilling and sustainable.

Leah says, "Using the Profitability Triangle as a lens through which to look at your business and choose your next move is a more meaningful approach than just tackling what's on your to-do list today."

Let's look at the Profitability Triangle a little closer. Financial profitability is fairly straightforward: bringing in enough money to sustain your needs and do the things you want to do for yourself, your family, and your business.

Professional profitability means doing work that you love and being known for the right things. Are people coming to you for your area of expertise? Are you working in your sweet spot or doing your

Highest Contribution? And do you have a full client pipeline so you can make decisions from a place of abundance instead of scarcity?

Leah suggests that the third type of profitability — emotional profitability — often gets overlooked, but is one of the most important when it comes to knowing what to focus on in your business without overwhelm and burnout. Emotional profitability asks: Are you having fun? Are you doing work you enjoy? Does this business fulfill you? Do you feel optimistic about the future?

You can use these three levers to assess your business and give you a clearer picture of where you need to focus. Perhaps increasing Financial Profitability means raising prices, increasing Professional Profitability means you need to focus on visibility, or increasing Emotional Profitability means creating systems to streamline less-enjoyable parts of your business.

Remember, there is not just one type of profitability! To learn more about this concept check out Leah at http://smartsgetspaid.com

FOCUS AFFIRMATION

YOUR IMPACT IS *inevitable*

CHAPTER 7:
MAKE TIME FOR DEEP WORK AND PRIORITIZE YOUR HIGHEST CONTRIBUTION

FOCUS ON THIS

- Deep Work is your most important work; it's the work that will make an impact and push your life forward.
- After being inspired by an idea, book or conversation, take the next step of scheduling and protecting time to work on that big idea.
- Having a filter question like "Will it make the boat go faster?" is a great way to see if your daily actions are leading to the results you want.

CHAPTER 8:

CLEARING THE DECK FOR FOCUS

The concept of using focus time to do non-Deep Work tasks can be a bit controversial. To make an impact and have time for your Highest Contribution you must set aside time to plan and to actually do the Deep Work. We argue that the third bucket, Clear the Deck, is as important for reaching your goals.

Clearing the Deck means strategically scheduling time to complete the nagging tasks that prevent you from doing more important work because they clutter your to-do list and your brain. Clearing the Deck may not seem to move you toward your goals, but this bucket clears mental space and energy for other work, and may help replenish and refresh you to do your Deep Work and bigger visioning.

Clean up your desk, call and schedule those appointments, order new supplies, follow up on invoices … all those things you keep thinking about when you try to do other work. Clearing the Deck might look like powering through emails that are distracting you from working on the big things, or cleaning your office so you can film videos later. It could look like crossing off a bunch of seemingly tiny tasks so you can put away work for the weekend and spend time with your family. Sometimes

Clearing the Deck means doing some self-care: finish that book that you can't put down or write a note to a friend.

It all boils down to setting yourself up for better focus later. The key is to keep your Clear the Deck in a specific container.

Here are some ways to use Clear the Deck Sessions:

- Check off as many to-dos as you can—Send invoices, pay bills, make a dentist appointment, order office supplies, research flights, buy a gift, write thank you notes, find your phone charger, make reservations ... Maybe your planning braindump left you with a bunch of lingering tasks that haven't been scheduled, or you were doing a Deep Work session and jotted down some smaller tasks for later. Schedule a focus block each week to keep this list under control.

- Clear out your inbox—Did email and mail pile up? Plow through it. You don't have to get to inbox zero, but delete things you don't need, reply to key messages, and make a list of follow up you need to do.

- Clean up your workspace—Sometimes after a big deadline or a busy week, you literally need to clear your desk, office, or workspace. File or recycle papers. Put pens, Post-its, and other supplies away. Wipe everything down. Set yourself up for work tomorrow.

- Wrap things up—You had a great call with a client, but need to send a follow up email. You did the Deep Work of creating something, but now you need to update your team on the progress you made. You need to file notes and send an invoice to close out a project. Use a Clear the Deck session to tie up those loose ends.

- Deal with finances—I talked about the idea of Financial Friday earlier, and this is a great regular Clear the Deck session to have on your calendar. Schedule time each week to pay bills, follow up on invoices, and go over your numbers. This helps you stay on top of this part of your business without getting distracted by other things that come up in your week.

These are also the tasks that can somehow take all day to complete if you let them. See the sidebar on Parkinson's Law. It states that "work expands so as to fill the time available for its completion." In other words, the amount of time a person allocates for a task will determine the amount of time it takes to complete the task, rather than the complexity of the task itself. By declaring, "I'll take the next 90 minutes to complete these Clear the Deck tasks," you can usually contain it to that 90-minute block, then move on to Deep Work or planning with your next block of focus time. Taking time to Clear the Deck can improve focus and energy for the new projects you want to start.

Sometimes our members report lower levels of focus when they set out to Clear the Deck, which makes sense. You're often doing many small tasks or tasks that have built in distraction. At the same time, our members also report getting a lot done in their Clear the Deck sessions. Having a container and accountability can help get things you are avoiding checked off your list.

While we recommend spending most of your Focus Time in the Planning and Visioning bucket or the Deep Work bucket, a regularly scheduled Clear the Deck can go a long way to helping you focus on your Highest Contribution without falling into overwhelm.

SIDEBAR: Parkinson's Law

Parkinson's Law is the idea that work expands to fill the time available for its completion. This concept suggests that when you have more time available, you tend to find ways to fill that time with additional tasks or activities.

Essentially, your perceived need for time expands to match the amount of time that you have available. This can lead to feelings of being overwhelmed or busy, even when you have ample time to complete your tasks.

If you have more time to complete a task, you will find ways to use that time, often resulting in the task taking longer than necessary. Conversely, if you set a smaller container, you can use Parkinson's Law to help you complete work faster.

If you give yourself eight hours to write a blog post, it will most likely take eight hours. You'll research more, edit longer, get lost looking at images, etc., but if you have one hour to write the blog post before a deadline, you'll most likely get it done in that timeframe.

This is not a reason to overpack your schedule, but sometimes by reasonably restricting the container, you can work more efficiently.

CHAPTER 8:
CLEARING THE DECK FOR FOCUS

FOCUS ON THIS

- Clear the Deck is about completing tasks that are distracting you from focus.
- Create a time container for your Clear the Deck tasks.
- Spend most of your focus time on Planning & Visioning or Deep Work, but strategically use Clear the Deck sessions to set yourself up to focus better during the other two buckets.

PART III

YOU HAVE EXACTLY THE TIME YOU NEED — FINDING TIME TO FOCUS

"Different people have different rhythms, and there is no single 'best' way to manage time."

Cal Newport

CHAPTER 9:

GET REALISTIC ABOUT TIME – HOW MUCH YOU HAVE AND HOW MUCH YOU NEED

You don't need more time, you need more focus.

I started my business when my daughter was an infant and while I was still working as an employee for someone else. I would create these huge to-do lists of things I needed to do for my business and at the end of the week, I would be so frustrated with myself for only accomplishing a handful of tasks. I felt I should be working harder and/or being more productive, but the truth was I was working at my day job while my kids were in school and daycare, and trying to start my business during my daughter's naps on the days I was home with her. That meant I had one or two 45-minute sprints, two days a week to run my business. My to-do list contained way more tasks than could fit in three hours, but I never looked at the math. I just thought I needed to "be better." Sound familiar?

When it comes to getting things done, it's easy to overestimate how much time we have and how quickly we can complete tasks. If we're not careful, that can lead to disappointment and frustration, and make us feel like we're constantly falling short of our goals. So often I hear people beat themselves up for not working hard enough or fast enough or somehow not being good at what they do, just because they didn't get "enough" done. (Ahem ... thank you capitalism for the constant push for productivity and success defined by the need to make more money, acquire more power, and achieve more status created by a system that values profit over people and leads to exploitation, inequality, and burnout ... but I digress.) If you are not getting "enough" done in the time you have available, are you really bad at productivity or are you choosing the wrong container to hold your tasks?

Soup and Time Management

Let me give you an analogy. Imagine you are making a huge pot of soup. You've gone to the farmers market and picked out the freshest organic ingredients and the perfect spices. You put everything in a six-quart stock pot, the All-Clad® one you got as a wedding gift. You simmer the soup all day, and it is delicious, the best soup you've ever made. Then, you try to pour the soup into a one-quart storage container. As you can imagine, the soup spills all over the floor. You look at the mess and say to yourself, "I'm not a very good cook."

It's easy to see in this example that the problem was not with your cooking skill, but with the size of the storage container you chose relative to the amount of soup you had. The same can be said about productivity. So often we will put 10 things on our to-do list and try to accomplish them all in the hour we have between client meetings. Then when we only get two or three done, we blame ourselves for not being productive enough, or focused enough, or frankly good enough to get it all done. But like the soup analogy, we have to pick the right sized container. If we have a six-quart pot filled with soup, we need six quart-size jars to store it all. If we have 10 things on our list that will each take 30 minutes, then we need time that adds up to five hours to accomplish those things.

Know How Long Tasks Will Take

Just like we try to put leftovers in too-small containers, we do that with time, too.

Humans are bad at estimating how long tasks will take. How often have you expected a task to take 10 or 15 minutes and it ends up taking you two hours? What about those things that you procrastinate for weeks because you think it will take you so long to complete and when you finally sit down to do it, you're done in a fraction of the time you were dreading?

Just like we need to get realistic about the time we have to complete our tasks, we also need to get a better understanding of how long tasks take us to complete. Although we can have surprises where something takes us less time than we had thought—this especially happens when we are in a state of focus—I find that tasks tend to take longer than we think they will. This is another reason that people tend to get overwhelmed by their to-do list or feel busy all the time, but don't feel like they're making a dent in the things that need to get done. We tend to drastically overestimate what we can get done in any given time period.

I recommend getting in the habit of not only creating a to-do list, but assigning an approximate time to each of the items on your to-do list. Then you can do the math to figure out if the time you need fits into the time you have. If you have five things on your to-do list and have 90 minutes before you have to pick your kids up from school, you might assume you can get them all done. Then, when you don't, you feel frustrated and discouraged. Instead of thinking you aren't productive enough or that you aren't working hard enough, really you probably haven't allotted the proper amount of time.

If you start by determining that the five items on your to-do list will each take 30 minutes to complete, adding up to two and a half hours of work, but then you realize that you have only an hour and a half of time, you can make a more intentional decision of which three tasks can get done and schedule the other two tasks for later. When you get to the end of your 90-minute block of time, you will be more likely to have completed those three items, leaving you feeling successful instead of downtrodden. Being more realistic not only means that you will have a better understanding of when and how things will get done, but you can be kinder to yourself in the process.

Edit blog post - 20 min

Find image - 30 min

Pay invoice - 15 min

Reply to DM - 30 min

Leave Buffer Time

Just like you need a little space for air in your soup container (you can't fill it right up to the rim), you need a little space in your calendar too. This is buffer time.

If you have a five-hour workday and five hours of tasks, you'll most likely end up frustrated that you didn't get everything done, because things don't always go according to plan. Meetings run long, kids get sick, and clients have emergencies.

What can you do to prevent this from happening? Round up or tack on a little time to each task when you schedule it. Make sure you also include time for things like eating, going to the bathroom, and answering email.

"But Megan... if I put buffer time on my calendar and plan to do fewer tasks each day, I'm going to get less done and everything is going to take longer."

Maybe. But if you can't realistically get things done in the time you try to force them into, are you really behind? What if you set a realistic expectation and build in buffer time so you can finish exactly what you wanted to? You'll feel better and build momentum to continue the work that's most important instead of overworking yourself and battling burnout.

3 Things You Probably Aren't Making Time For

Your Highest Contribution, white space, downtime: you need time for them all ... and none of them are the same as buffer time.

In addition to trying to pack too much into a small container, we routinely leave something out of that container altogether. When you feel like you don't have time, it's easy to leave out time for your Highest Contribution, white space, and downtime. To get real about time, you need to set aside dedicated time for all of these things.

Highest Contribution

My clients often say that they need more open time on their calendar or they need more focus time. They spend the majority of their days responding to others, whether that is their client's needs, their team's questions, or their family's care. They are busy all day, but when they get to the end of a day, they don't feel like they have done the important things, the things that will move their business forward. Often when we feel this way, it's because we have lost sight of what our Highest Contribution is in our businesses. Remember, our Highest Contribution moves us toward the impact we want to make.

You need to set aside dedicated time on your calendar for this Highest Contribution. This is the time you do the thing only you can do. You write the content, you create the art, you develop the program. Maybe your Highest Contribution in your business right now is talking about your business, or maybe your Highest Contribution is being interviewed on podcasts or talking with potential investors. Your Highest Contribution can shift over the year or over the life of your business, but I can assure you that your Highest Contribution is not approving a website font or processing a customer refund. Not that those things don't need to get done (and maybe you are the person to do them), but they can't happen at the expense of time spent in your Highest Contribution. You need dedicated time on your calendar for your Highest Contribution — and you have to protect that time.

Now possibly the most important thing about the time you set aside for your Highest Contribution? It is not buffer time. Let me repeat. The time you have blocked out for your Highest Contribution is not the time that gets eaten into when your task takes longer than planned or your client needs an emergency session. You need separate time for both. Buffer time helps you protect your Highest Contribution time.

White Space

What do Einstein, Bill Gates, and Sheryl Sandburg all have in common? They all intentionally put white space time on their calendars. The idea is to carve out periods of unstructured time for reflection, planning, and thinking, which can help boost productivity, creativity, and well-being. We're going to talk all about this later, but know that it is scientifically proven that white space on your calendar will make you more successful. Intrigued? Stay tuned.

White space may feel dispensable, but you need it. To other people, it may look like open space where they can schedule with you or get your help, but that's what buffer time is for. White Space is for higher-level work, like brainstorming new ideas, solving problems, and visioning the future of your company and your life, not for completing tasks. Don't use your white space to "finish" things that didn't get done or to put out fires.

Downtime

A client recently told me she is so busy managing her team that she saves her important work for evenings and weekends when her team isn't working. Now the beauty of being an entrepreneur is you can work whenever you want, but you can't work all the time. That's Hustle Culture again. (We'll talk more about work hours in the next chapter.)

You need downtime. You need time for rest, for hobbies, for self-care. Downtime is its own category and it's not work time. Downtime shouldn't be your buffer time or your Highest Contribution time (even though your Highest Contribution excites you). Not only do you need downtime to stay healthy, happy, and out of burnout, but your downtime is probably not your "Grade A time." We'll talk more about Grade A time later, but for now think about your best time to get your important work done and when you'd prefer to be in the garden or horizontal on the couch with a romance novel. They likely aren't the same time of day.

When you build in buffer time, prioritize your Highest Contribution, and include white space and downtime in your calendar, you are rejecting Hustle Culture, which tells you that you don't have enough time, or that productivity has to come at the cost of your mental health. When you get realistic about your time, you will start to see that you have exactly the time that you need.

If it still sounds impossible to fit it all in, don't worry. This is where focus comes in, and the rest of this book will help you do exactly that.

Focus In Action: Dr. Sheree Bryant Sekou

I had attended virtual coworking in the past to get important work done, but there was one huge missing ingredient — and that was planning. While virtual coworking allowed me to get my work done, weekly planning really enabled me to be much more intentional about prioritizing my most important projects and related tasks.

I am also more gentle with my scheduling. I am offering myself more spaciousness. I plan not just work, but things that are not related to work. I didn't want to look at my calendar and have it completely jam packed, so I appreciated the grace and gentleness to block off days for rest, relaxation, personal sabbath, all of those things are really important to me. And I'm doing a much better job of that by putting planning on the top of my to-do list on Mondays and then getting to work after that.

In terms of what I've been able to accomplish, it's making sure I get the non-work time in there as well to prevent some of the workstuff from creeping into my personal time. The intentionality and planning for it at the beginning of the week vs. kind of seeing what happens has been a game changer for me. I don't miss a Monday planning session if possible.

FOCUS AFFIRMATION

YOU HAVE
exactly
THE TIME YOU NEED

CHAPTER 9:
GET REALISTIC ABOUT TIME — HOW MUCH YOU HAVE AND HOW MUCH YOU NEED

FOCUS ON THIS

- Just like making soup requires choosing the right size storage container, time management is all about choosing the right container for the tasks you have.
- Build in buffer time for when things run long or emergencies come up.
- Highest Contribution, white space, and downtime are not all the same thing, and none of them should be used as buffer time.

CHAPTER 10:

DEFINE YOUR CONTAINER

The beauty of being an entrepreneur is flexibility, right? But that is the rub, too. If you have a schedule where you could work 24 hours a day, 7 days a week, you can start to feel like you should be working 24 hours a day, 7 days a week. This leads to feeling like you're constantly in the wrong place at the wrong time. Pushing your kid on the swing? You should be replying to that client. Finishing up this week's blog post at 10 p.m.? You really should get in bed.

The solution? Define your container. Set start and end times to your work day.

If this book were titled *One Way to Be More Focused*, my suggestion would be to set work hours.

You need to know when your work day starts and when it ends. That is the only way you can strategically plan what you can get done. Remember our soup analogy? Setting work hours is picking your storage container before you even shop for ingredients. It's looking at the two-quart storage container you have first and deciding to make just enough soup to fit in the container you already have. Deciding the size of your work container first is the best way to ensure everything fits into your schedule, and soup (or work, in this case) doesn't spill all over the counter.

Your hours can be set like Monday through Thursday 9 a.m. to 4 p.m., or they can be flexible each week, or even change each day, but at the beginning of each day you need a clear plan for when your work day starts and when it stops.

Your work hours shouldn't be "all the free time I have." If your kids are in school from 9 to 2, your work hours do not need to be 9 to 2. If you usually eat dinner at 6, your work day can still end at 4. In fact, giving yourself a more realistic container will actually make you more productive in the time you have. If you say, "My kids are in school from 9 to 2, so those are my work hours," but then you come home from drop off, refill your coffee, send a quick text to a parent you ran into at school, pull out frozen meat to thaw for dinner, and now its 9:30, you are behind. You have now "wasted" part of your work day, and if you have planned to get five hours of work done, you have the added stress of getting caught up. Maybe your work day should be 10 to 2.

How to Set Work Hours

The first step in creating your container is to decide what your ideal total work hours are. This can be done a few different ways. You might clearly have a number in your head like, I'd like to limit my work hours to 30 hours a week. You might have outside restrictions, like your kids' school schedule, that help you say, "I have 20 hours a week while the kids are in school." If you are untangling from a schedule where you work in "all available gaps of time" you might need to do a little journaling and time-tracking to figure out your available work hours.

You can also back into how much time you have available by doing some math. Everyone starts with 168 hours in a week.

Ask yourself these questions to help you narrow down how you want to spend yours:

1. How much sleep do I need/want? From what time to what time?
2. How much time do I need to wind down and prepare for sleep?
3. How much time do I need in the mornings to get ready for my day? (Think about not only things like getting dressed, showering, etc., but also meditation, morning pages, or anything else you want to include in your morning routine.)
4. How much time do I need for meal preparation and eating?
5. Do I want my work hours to include weekends, or only Monday through Friday?
6. How much time do I want to block out for exercise or movement?
7. How much time do I set aside for family and friends? (This can be caring for children, spending time with a spouse, or gathering with friends.)
8. What else needs time in my schedule (pet care, volunteer work, social activities, commuting, etc.)?

Once you have numbers for each of these, start subtracting from 168. What's left over is your available work time. It can also be helpful to visually do this on a weekly planning page. You can download a blank version at http://focus-sessions.com/bookbonus.

Here is my preferred method to decide work hours: Sit down with a journal and make a wish list, or really listen to your own intuition about what you would like your days to look like. This is your time to think about things like fitting in your favorite yoga class Mondays at noon, or always finishing your work by 3 p.m. Perhaps you want to plan to work one weekend a month so you can have more flexibility during your week. Maybe you want to have one late work night a week when your partner is responsible for dinner. Or maybe you never want to miss volunteering at the animal shelter on Thursdays. These ideas will help you create a work schedule that is aligned with the house you want to build we discussed in Part 1. The key is really thinking about how you want to feel. Do you feel better when you get started early? Are you more fulfilled when you get self-care and family things done first? I find when I focus on how I want my week to feel, my work hours naturally start to take shape.

Try asking yourself the following questions:

- When do I want my work day to start to feel the best?
- When do I want my work day to end?
- Do I want some days to be longer than others?
- Do I want a day to meet up with friends?
- Do I have other important things to do during my week like an exercise class or volunteering?
- Is my work week M–F or weekends, too?

Remember, there are no ideal work hours. Start at 6 a.m.? Great! Don't start until 3 p.m.? Perfect. Never work on Tuesdays? Wonderful. Don't do friend lunches midday so you can stop work in time for school pick up? Great, schedule weekend friend-hikes instead! Remember, Focus Culture is all about regaining control of our calendars.

However you arrive at it, having a sense of when your workday starts and when it stops, as well as how many total hours you have during the week to work, will help with all the other planning you need to do. And don't worry — your work schedule and hours can (and probably will) change! You might be in a season where your family takes more time and your work hours are less. Or perhaps this quarter you want to work more hours so you can take time off during the summer. Maybe it's your busy season in your industry, so your work hours look different than they do during your off season. I recommend revisiting your work hours every 90 days or so.

Create Opening and Closing Routines

Once you know when you work, make sure your brain knows too. How do you tell your brain it's time to switch into work mode? **Use routines as triggers to tell your brain it's time to start your work day.** By creating an event or series of events that always happen before you start (or end) your work day, your brain will start to associate that event with getting into the mode to do your best work (or turn off for the night).

Opening Routines

While most people think of a morning routine being about the things you do first upon waking up (which is great, and I recommend that too), I love to think of a startup or Opening Routine for my workday. Most people have to switch hats a few times in the morning. You might start out with the personal care hat: getting dressed, working out, meditating, or even just using the restroom. Then you might have to roll into family mode: getting kids fed, dressed, and out the door, or tending to animals or other household chores. You might expect your brain to switch instantly into work mode. You sit down at your laptop, but you might get distracted by the breakfast dishes or an email from your child's school.

By creating an Opening Routine to your work day, you trigger your brain to switch from family caretaker role to business mode.

Your Opening Routine could happen at 6 a.m., 10 a.m., or even 2 p.m., whenever your work day begins. Think about the things you want to do to signal the start of your workday, before diving into email, to set up your brain to do its best work all day.

Perhaps the first thing you do when you sit at your desk is take 10 deep breaths, or pull an oracle card to guide your day. Maybe you signal the start of your day by wiping down your work surface with a pleasant smelling wipe. (This was mine for the years I worked at my dining room table. My coconut cleansing wipes signaled my brain that my work day was about to start, and the wiping down ensured I didn't put my laptop in a leftover smear of syrup from breakfast.) Maybe your workday starts by doing some yoga poses next to your desk, reciting an affirmation, or starting a fresh list of the day's tasks.

Your Opening Routine can take 30 minutes or 30 seconds. But by repeating a defined action each day, your brain will know it's time to transition and get down to business.

Closing Routines

Do you ever wake up in a panic at 3 a.m. thinking about something important you need to be sure to do the next day?

A Closing Routine solved this problem for me (most of the time).

I realized that the panic at 3 a.m. was because my brain was afraid I was going to forget something important. Now, at the end of my work day, I have a Closing Routine that helps me avoid this panic thinking.

I reserve 15 minutes at the end of my work day to review what has been done that day, celebrate my wins, check my calendar for the next day, and write out a fresh to-do list of the most important tasks for the next day (and even schedule those onto my calendar if I can). Then I close my computer, straighten my desk, take the dishes to the kitchen (how many different beverage vessels does one need in a day?), plug in my devices to charge, recycle note paper, and otherwise set myself up to start work the next day.

This way I can "shut down" my brain for the night knowing that I have captured my most important ideas and to-dos for the next day ... and know that a cat won't knock my half-empty water glass all over my computer overnight.

When I do wake up in the middle of the night, I remind myself, "You've already set aside time to do that thing tomorrow," and I can fall back asleep.

Set your Opening and Closing Routines

On the following pages, you'll find a list of possible Opening and Closing activities. Remember, for it to act as a trigger, it needs to be something you do consistently without fail. So start small and be reasonable. While you might wish to start each work day with a 10 minute meditation, if it's not something you consistently do, make your opening routine something simpler that you always do, like three deep breaths or lighting a candle. That becomes your trigger to start your day. You can still build a meditation practice, but your trigger isn't dependent on something new.

Same with your Closing Routine. Perhaps your closing trigger is simply clearing off your desk and putting all your pens back in the pencil can or blowing out that candle. Something you can consistently do. You can always add to it as it becomes routine.

Look over the list on the next page and pick out things you want to do to signal the start and end of your work day. Then turn the page and create your own Opening and Closing routines.

There is also space for this in your *Focused Workbook*.

Opening Routine Ideas:

- Drink some water & fill water bottle
- Move your body (workout/yoga/walk/stretch)
- Get a cup of coffee/tea/green juice
- Meditate
- Journal
- Gratitude practice
- Pull a mantra or oracle card
- Check daily metrics
- Check in with revenue goals
- Write down top 3 priorities
- Review project management (ie. Asana/Clickup)
- Check team communications (ie. Slack)
- Send morning update to team
- Create today's detailed to-do list
- Clear/process email inbox
- Clear/process physical inbox
- Review quarter goals
- Read visualizations
- Today's meal plan
- Review calendar
- Highlight today's work time
- Water plants
- Clear desk
- Other Ideas:

____

____

____

____

____

Sample Opening Routine:

Start Time:	8:30am
Drink Water	0 min
Gratitude	5 min
3 top priorities	10 min
Check Asana	15 min
Total Time:	30 min
End Time:	9:00am

Closing Routine Ideas:

- Clear/process email inbox
- Clear/process physical inbox
- Check tomorrow's calendar
- Close out project management (ie. Asana/ Clickup)
- Migrate incomplete to-do's
- Write out tomorrow's to-do's
- Write down a win from today
- Check team communications (ie. Slack)
- Check out with team
- Meditate
- Journal
- Gratitude practice
- Check daily metrics
- Review calendar
- Tomorrow's meal plan
- Move your body (workout/yoga/walk/ stretch)
- Clear desk
- Tidy office
- Water plants
- Take cups/water bottles/ dishes to kitchen
- Shut off computer
- Turn off work-related notifications
- Pull a mantra or oracle card
- Other Ideas:

____

____

____

____

____

Sample Closing Routine:

Start Time:	4:30pm
Check Asana	10 min
Write a Win	5 min
Slack Check-out	5 min
Clear Desk	10 min
Total Time:	30 min
End Time:	5:00pm

My Opening Routine:

Start Time: ____________

☐ ____________

☐ ____________

☐ ____________

☐ ____________

☐ ____________

☐ ____________

Total Time: ____________

End Time: ____________

My Closing Routine:

Start Time: ____________

☐ ____________

☐ ____________

☐ ____________

☐ ____________

☐ ____________

☐ ____________

Total Time: ____________

End Time: ____________

CHAPTER 10:
DEFINE YOUR CONTAINER

FOCUS ON THIS

- Setting work hours is my single most important system for making time for focus.
- You get to define your work hours. Start early or start late. It's all about what works best for you.
- Create an Opening and Closing Routine to signal to your brain that it's time to start and end your work day.

CHAPTER 11:

YOUR UNIQUE FOCUS FORMULA

You know that focus is important. That's probably why you're reading this book! I know that focus is important. Heck, my team and I built an entire business around it! Focus is the key to getting your Most Important Work done and making the impact you want to make, but **our brains are not designed to focus all the time.** In fact, research shows that excessive focus actually drains our energy, leads to a breakdown of our ability to make good decisions, and leads to more impulsivity.

So how long should you focus at a given stretch? While everyone is different, and so much influences your ability to focus at any given time, the human brain is really only designed to focus for at most 2 hours. Some research shows that the ideal period of focus might be more like 50 minutes. In fact, the Pomodoro Method of working for 25 minutes, taking a quick break, then working for another 25 minutes was designed around that research. After about an hour of intense focus, you need a break.

This reinforces the idea of setting up a schedule that allows for periods of specific focus time and periods of less-focused work time, and periods of white space, downtime, or deliberately unfocused time.

The Importance of NOT Focusing

Ever wonder why your best ideas come in the shower or while you're out on a hike? One theory is that you need time when you're actively focusing, and time when you're not. During this time when you are not actively focusing, your brain enters the Default Mode Network (DMN). The DMN is a network of brain regions that are active when you're not actively engaged in a task. This network is involved in things like memory consolidation, self-reflection, and creativity. When you're constantly in a state of focus, you're essentially shutting down the DMN, which can lead to feelings of burnout and decreased productivity.

When you allow yourself to take non-focus time, you're giving the DMN a chance to come back online. This is where your brain revisits old data, rearranges ideas, draws on memories, predicts outcomes, and even tunes into other people's ideas. During this time, you may come up with creative solutions and new ideas that would not have been possible if you tried to force an extended period of focus.

I asked a group of clients what they needed more of in their day to make the impact they wanted to make, and many of them instinctively said "white space." They were listening to their intuition, but they were neurologically correct, too. Your brain needs that white space or time when you're doing low-key activities like gardening, knitting, or showering to activate the DMN. Intentional time spent in this "white space" is shown to increase creativity, build leadership skills, and even re-energize the brain for another focus session.

How can you incorporate non-focus time into your daily routine? One of the simplest ways is to take regular breaks throughout the day to relax and do something that doesn't require much focus. This could be something as simple as taking a short walk, reading a book, or just sitting and looking out the window. You could also try activities that are known to activate the DMN, such as meditation, yoga, or journaling.

The point is, if you feel like you "can't focus for very long" or you should be getting back to focusing after an unintentional break, know that your brain is taking care of itself and even benefiting from NOT focusing all the time, even when Hustle Culture is telling you that something is wrong.

Decide How Much Focus Time You Need

You have now set your work hours, and you've learned that your brain is not designed to focus all the time. Now it's time to plan how much of your set work hours should be spent in focus time. How much focus time you need depends largely on how you plan to use your focus time, because different tasks require different levels of focus.

As part of our Focus Sessions framework, we block off 90-minute virtual coworking sessions. At the beginning of each session, the Focus Session facilitators encourage each participant to not only declare what they're working on, but to define it in one of our three time buckets: Planning, Deep Work, or Clearing the Deck.

Like we established in Part II, the majority of our focus time should be in deep work or our Most Important Work. But how much is that? Let's do a little math to get even more clear. For the sake of simplicity, let's start with this equation: **10–15% of your total work hours should prioritize your Most Important Work,** so a 30 hour work week would need three to four-and-a-half dedicated hours. If you are attending one of our Focus Sessions or creating your own 90-minute block, this means in a 30-hour work week, you should block out two to three Focus Sessions to get your Most Important Work done.

The amount of focused time you need depends on how you're using the time. Knowing that my brain has limited capacity to focus for extended periods of time, I like to block off a daily 90-minute session and dedicate it to one of the three time buckets. One for Planning to kick off my week, one for Clearing the Deck of nagging tasks to wrap up my week, and two to three Deep Work sessions. This still leaves me with over 20 hours a week to do all the other things that I need to do in my business, like meet with clients, meet with my team, and complete other administrative work.

You can also use focus time for things you might otherwise procrastinate. Many of our Focus Sessions members participate in Financial Friday, where they have a dedicated time to take care of their taxes and other financial matters every week. Setting aside a recurring Focus Session on Fridays to attend to the finances of your business means you don't have to think about it during the week if you know you have time reserved on Friday. (If it's already on the calendar, that's one less anxious thought to wake you up at 3 a.m.!)

The way you use the hours of focus time you need can change depending on what you are working on. While I was writing this book, I would block out six Focus Sessions a week over a six-week period dedicated to getting words on the page. Clearly it worked, because you are reading the finished book!

Understand Your Best Time for Focus

There is a lot of social pressure around when the "best" time of the day to work or be productive. It's all BS. We are all unique people with unique internal clocks and we are not pre-programmed with a specific time for productivity. So many common beliefs around work, like "The early bird gets the worm," and even an 8-5 work day come from a capitalistic, patriarchal model based around the agricultural and factory-based industries. Factory owners and farmers needed all their workers on the same schedule to maximize productivity and to take advantage of daylight. Turning work hours into a moral principle made it easier to get a society to work on the same schedule and work hour enforcements became about moral righteousness.

But this idea wasn't true for the factory workers then, and it's not true now. Especially as an entrepreneur, the best time to work is when it is the best time for YOU. You don't get a gold star for starting your day at 5 a.m., and you are not lazy if you don't start your day until noon. In fact, people who structure their work days around their own rhythms and energy levels are often more productive, and usually happier, than those who try to fit into a social norm.

The hours that you work are not a moral principle.

It's really important for you to understand that your best focus time might be different than the social norms. It might be different than your neighbor or your sister or one of your work colleagues. If your best focus time is 6 a.m., that's great, but if your best focus time is 2 p.m. or 8:00 p.m. that's great, too. There's no reason that you have to focus at a certain time of day or a certain point of the week. You may find that it's better for you to get all of those nagging tasks done early in the week and put your focus time in on Thursday and Friday, or maybe it's best for you to do your focus time first thing in the morning and then move on to other tasks later in your day.

Know that your best focus time can change throughout the day, the month, the seasons of the year, the seasons of life, and the lifecycle of your business. When you have a newborn, early morning focus time may be non-existent. When that baby becomes a teenager and rarely emerges before 11 a.m., mornings might become your best time for focus. Only you can determine the best time for your focus, and that might take a little thinking, a little tracking, and some trial and error.

Map Your Energy

You'll learn about the science behind why everyone has different levels of focus and motivation during the day, month, and year, but at the heart of it, know everyone is different and has unique times that are best to focus, work, rest, socialize, and do all the things. The very best thing you can do is to pay attention to what works for you. I recommend doing an energy mapping exercise any time you are feeling like you're not totally in your perfect groove when it comes to your use of productive time and downtime. There are all sorts of apps and bullet journal spreads for this, but a simple legal pad or a page in your journal works just as well.

Try this simple energy mapping method to start, then adapt as needed. Every two hours give yourself an energy score from 1-5. There is a blank energy map in your *Focused Workbook* for you to fill out.

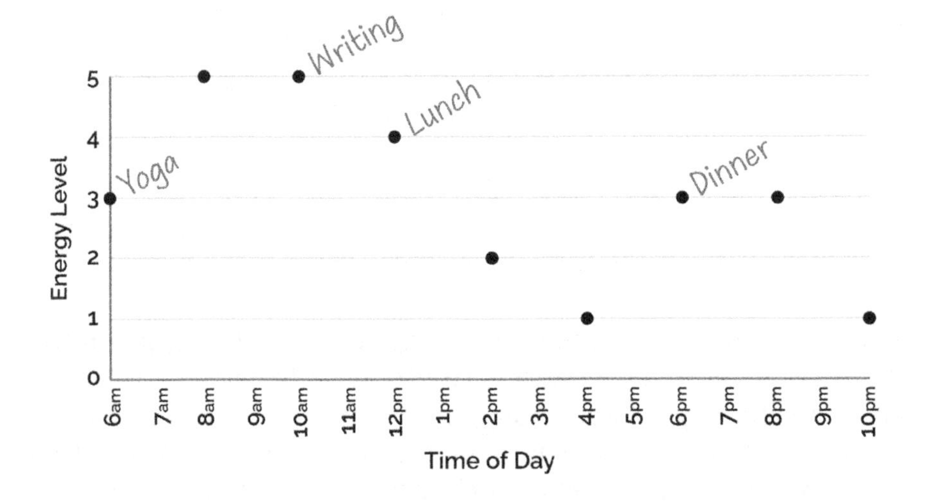

Do the exercise for three to four days, then look for patterns. Does your energy drop as the day goes on? Or do you need time to ramp up to your higher energy time?

If you want to dive in deeper, track more details when you give yourself your energy score. Each time you write down your score, take a few other notes about what you were doing in the time since your last score. Are your higher energy scores related to certain activities like taking a walk outside or having a snack? How about lower scores? Does a difficult client in the afternoon drain your energy? You can also note other things like how you slept the night before or what you ate to see if that affects your energy as well.

Once you have this data, you can start to plan your days around your own unique energy map. If you know you feel the most energy early in the morning after a walk, then you can plan your tasks that need the most focus for that time. If you know your energy dips after lunch, but also after difficult clients, maybe don't schedule them in that slot. (Or maybe do schedule them in that time slot if they are going to drain your energy anyway!)

The Business of Focus: Jackie Johnstone on Working Your Way

Jackie Johnstone is a Human Design expert for business owners. She looks at how our innate inner workings are unique to us and therefore make running our businesses unique. She tells us we are perfectly designed (one of my favorite sayings!).

Jackie explained that when she was approaching burnout in her marketing business, she thought there was something wrong with her, that she wasn't cut out for business. When she learned about Human Design and how each person has unique ways of working, communicating, collaborating, etc., it made more sense than traditional one-size-fits all business advice.

She tells us that we are perfectly designed to do the work we are here to do. We have all been given the exact combination of skills,traits,strengths, and attributes in our individual human design to accomplish that work. Some of us are programmed to work well in collaboration, and others are better suited to work alone. Some people really thrive with a high level of personal connection, so if they try to run a business that is more hands-off, it's not going to feel as aligned for them, even if the "gurus" tell them that is the way to scale. For some people, needing to make a decision on the spot is very uncomfortable, where others thrive with a fast-paced environment. Too often we shame ourselves into thinking we should be able to work another way.

Jackie tells us: "Remember that you are perfectly designed, there is no one right way to do any of this. Pay attention to what makes your body feel expansive, lit up, open. What are you being pulled towards? Pay attention to what feels heavy or contracted. That is your body's wisdom giving you the tools. You already know what is going to work best for you."

Find more on Jackie at http://jackiejohnstone.ca

Create Days, Months, and Seasons That Flow with Your Energy

The more you know about your own energy, the more you can work with it and not get frustrated when your brain seems to be working against you. You are unique; your schedule can be too.

Grade A time

Grade A time is that sweet spot of the day when your brain's ability to focus is at its peak and potential distractions are at their lowest.

Grade A time is different for everyone because of the variety of individual brain biology and lifestyles. If you've done the energy mapping exercise above, you'll have an idea of your Grade A time. You might find your focus is at its peak earlier in the day and distractions are the lowest right after you drop your kids off for school, so maybe your Grade A time is 9 a.m. Or you may find that 6 a.m. is an ideal time for you to do your Most Important Work before your team starts their day. Or perhaps you get a burst of focus energy after a long hike and eating lunch, meaning your Grade A time is at 1 p.m. Or maybe you get a second wind in the evening and find you can focus later after the world goes to sleep. You crank out your best work at 10 p.m.

Your Grade A time doesn't have to look like anyone else's, and your Grade A time may switch over the course of a year or over years. If you have young children at home, your Grade A time might be different than when they get older. Or your Grade A time might look different in the summer months than the winter. Knowing your Grade A time is the first step in protecting it and using it for your Grade A tasks, which is another way to say, your Most Important Work.

Grade A tasks go in Grade A time. While it might be convenient to stop at the grocery store after dropping your kids off at school, if you know that 9 a.m. is your best time for focus, save the shopping trip for another time. Or if you know you can get your Most Important Work done right after lunch, put the Do Not Disturb on your Slack channel so you don't get distracted by questions from your team members.

Because Grade A time is meant to be the time when your brain focuses best, remember that your blocks of Grade A time shouldn't be longer than two hours at most. So if you're feeling guilty for not being available to others during your Grade A time, remember this is a limited time window. Giving yourself a 90-minute block of time to focus on your Most Important Work will move your projects forward further and faster than trying to dip in and out of project time while also being available for your kids, your team, your clients, or anything else.

Hormones and Focusing Monthly

You might find your focus changes not only over the course of a day, but over the course of a month. This is especially true for people who menstruate or who have higher levels of estrogen in their system. In fact, understanding your 28-day hormonal cycle can be a powerful tool for understanding your focus and productivity. By understanding the different phases of the cycle and the hormonal changes that occur during each phase, you can plan around, or at least be aware of these changes in energy levels.

The menstrual cycle is divided into four phases: the menstrual phase, the follicular phase, the ovulatory phase, and the luteal phase. Each phase is characterized by different hormonal changes, which can have a significant impact on energy levels, mood, and cognitive abilities.

During the menstrual phase, levels of estrogen and progesterone are low, which can lead to feelings of fatigue and low energy. This is a good time to focus on rest and self-care, rather than trying to tackle demanding projects or tasks. This can also

Focus In Action: Samantha Crockett

As someone who has worked for a long time to make their ADHD work for them, Focus Planning was a piece of the puzzle to finally making peace with my brain and moving forward in productive ways. Before Focus Sessions, I tried *everything* to implement routines or track tasks/projects and nothing worked. I made complicated lists, I set alarms, I tried morning routines, I lived moment to moment. Focus Sessions came along at the right time in my life for it to have such a huge impact, and I cannot imagine going back to "the before times" anymore. I've just learned too much.

I love knowing that Focus Sessions are there when I need them, for exactly what I need them for. Having a community of people to talk with about planning really helps me figure out what works for me and what doesn't, and keeps me on track

Since joining Focus Sessions, I've really embraced a the non-negotiable things that help keep my day on track. I feel significantly better about my ADHD, anxiety, and executive functioning issues and see them as much more normal and okay, because Focus Sessions have taught me that there really isn't one way to get sh*t done. I find myself significantly more committed to my business because I no longer feel overwhelmed by all the stuff it requires.

Learn more about Samantha: http://enthusiastic-neighbor.com or http://enthusiasticsamantha.com.

be a good time to organize and purge. As your body is going through a shedding and a fresh start it can be a good time to do that mentally or with your space as well.

The follicular phase, which begins after the menstrual phase, is characterized by an increase in estrogen levels. You might feel more energized and inspired during this time. This can lead to improved focus and concentration, making it a good time to tackle complex tasks or projects that require a lot of mental energy.

The ovulatory phase, which occurs around day 14 of the cycle, is characterized by a spike in estrogen and luteinizing hormone. This can lead to increased confidence, creativity, and sociability, making it a good time to network, attend meetings, or work on projects that involve collaboration.

Finally, the luteal phase, which begins after ovulation, is characterized by an increase in progesterone levels. This can lead to feelings of fatigue and irritability, and make it more difficult to focus and concentrate. This is a good time to spend on more routine or administrative tasks, rather than trying to tackle new projects or big challenges. If you spend time client-facing or in team meetings, think about if it might be better to schedule calls when you are not feeling as irritable.

While it might not always be possible to plan around the phases in your cycle, if you have power over your work schedule or when you schedule launches and the like, you can use this knowledge to adjust tasks with the days you have the right mindset and energy levels for performing them. This will help boost productivity and best utilize your skills. At the very least it can give you some grace around why you don't feel the same level of motivation all the time.

(It's important to note that every person's hormonal cycle is different, and some may not experience the same symptoms as others. But being aware of these phases and tracking your own menstrual cycle and its symptoms can help you understand how it impacts you.)

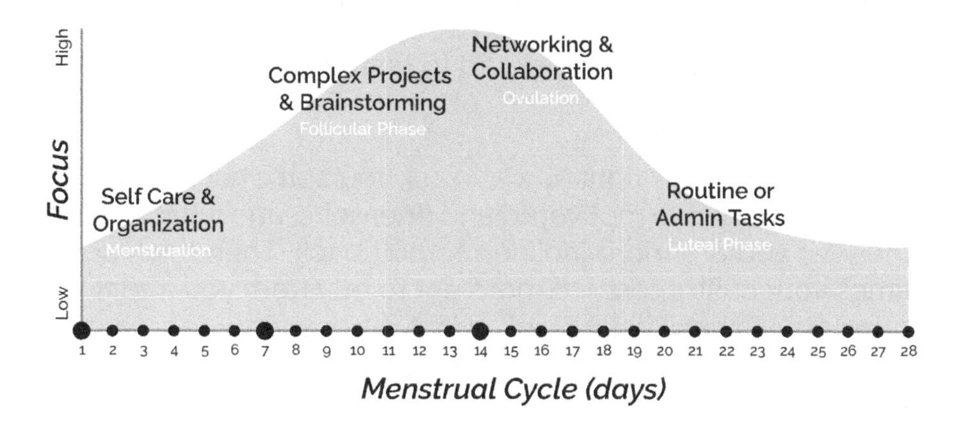

Planning Your Year or Your Seasons

Humans are cyclical beings and don't feel the same through the year. Some changes are based on nature, industry trends, and the schedules of the rest of the world. Just like individuals have times of the day or month they feel more motivated, more creative, and more productive, the same is true for the year.

Trees aren't always producing fruit, and you shouldn't be expected to either! If you look at the seasons, there is a time to plant seeds, time for things to grow and produce, time to harvest the fruits of hard work, and time for rest. So if you feel a little slower in the winter months and are more ready to do your "New Year's Planning" in March than in January, you are right on time with the seasons.

Planning your time throughout the year might be determined by your industry. Perhaps you have a busy season around the holidays and are quiet after the first of the year. Or perhaps you plan your time based on the school calendar with bigger pushes in October and February, and slower time over the summer and winter breaks.

There are times in the year you will feel more motivated or more excited to work harder and push, and there are times where you naturally feel more inclined to rest, think, or regroup. And all of this is okay.

Take a few minutes right now and ask yourself what times of the year you feel more motivated and energetic, and what times of the year you are more inclined to pull back. Then think about times your customers are more apt to buy from you and times sales are slower. Lastly, think about other schedules – a partner, a kid, or even your town's tourist flow – that impact when you want to be working harder and when you want to plan for slower times or time off. Fill out the following timeline with the peaks and valleys of your work year from an energy, scheduling, and business perspective. (You'll find this worksheet at http://focus-sessions.com/bookbonus for you to download for yourself.)

Plan Your Year

When it comes to managing your time, there's no one-size-fits-all solution. Everyone works differently and has unique habits, so it's important to figure out what works for you instead of blindly following what society tells you is the "right" way to do things. The key to being productive and making the most of your time is to understand your personal working style and set up a schedule that suits you. Trust me, breaking away from the norm and doing things your own way can lead to some seriously good results.

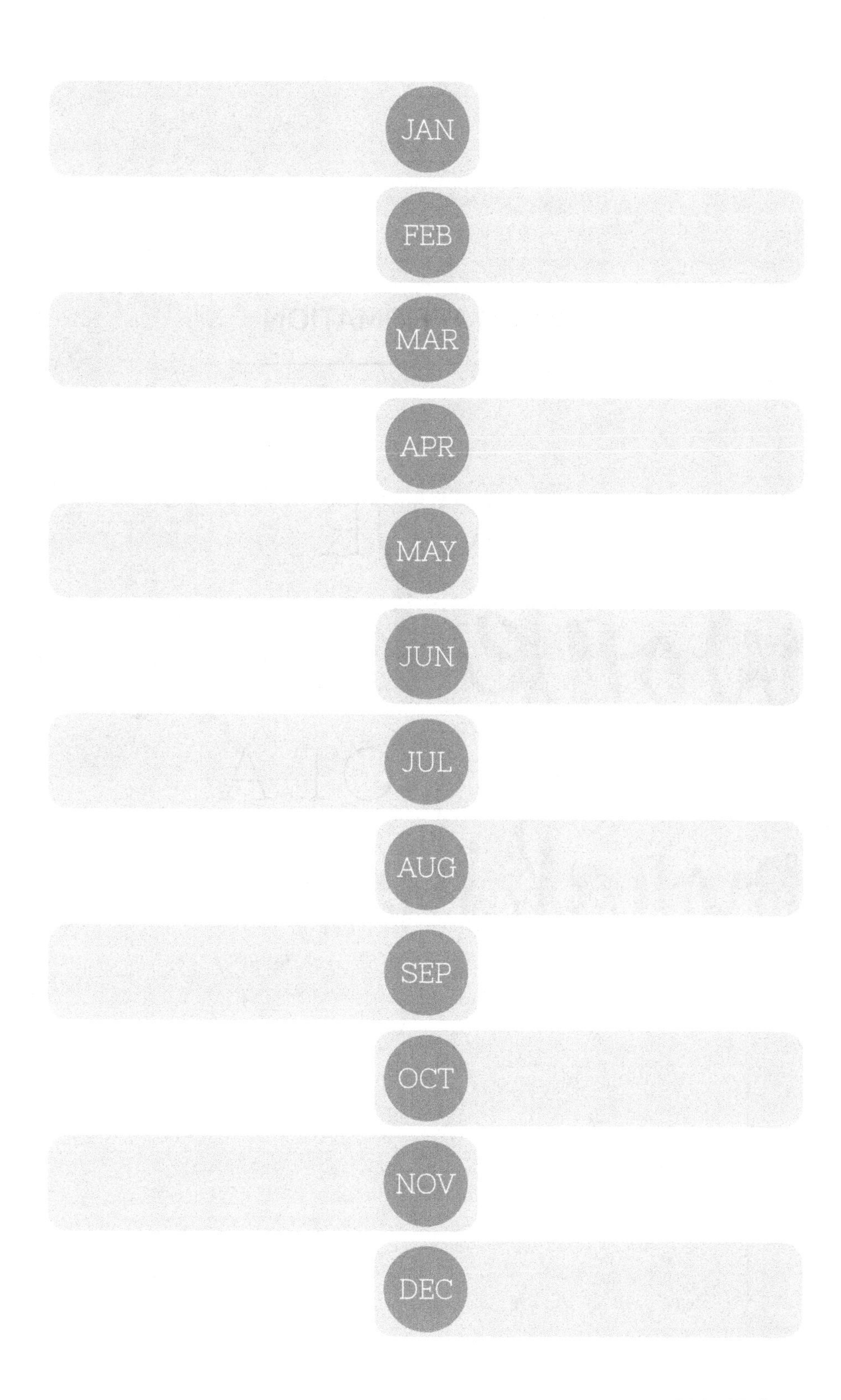
JAN
FEB
MAR
APR
MAY
JUN
JUL
AUG
SEP
OCT
NOV
DEC

FOCUS AFFIRMATION

YOUR *work hours* ARE NOT A *moral judgment*

CHAPTER 11:
YOUR UNIQUE FOCUS FORMULA

FOCUS ON THIS

- The Default Mode Network is activated when you are not actively focusing. Taking time to do low-key activities has been shown to increase creativity and re-energize the brain.
- Your work hours are not a moral principle. We all have unique best times for focus, and it might be different than what works for others around you.
- Your energy can change throughout the day, month, and year. Map your own energy to better understand your personal energy flow and how that affects focus.

CHAPTER 12:

SET UP A SCHEDULE THAT WORKS FOR YOU

Once you have mapped your energy, you can use that information to set your days and weeks up to work with your energy instead of against it.

One of the main reasons I went into business for myself and a main reason I hear from my clients that they did — is the flexibility to set my own work schedule. However, it's common for entrepreneurs to recreate traditional work schedules, or even a schedule that looks more like a class schedule from college! Or, in an effort to remain as unscheduled as possible, some people resist making a schedule or a plan at all in order to stay flexible.

Let's look at some different ways to set up a schedule that mixes flexibility, your own energy map, and more focus.

Create a Weekly Work Flow

Do you ever sit down at your desk and wonder, "What am I supposed to be doing right now?" Do you just jump into all the things? You sit down to write a proposal, but an email notification pops up and while you are responding, you wonder what you should make for dinner. When you sit back down to work on the proposal, you wonder if you should check in on that client ... When are you going to get it all done?

You love being an entrepreneur, but you can't help but daydream about someone else telling you exactly what you should be doing at any given moment. That's kind of what a Weekly Work Flow is. It's a gift your past self gives your present self so you know exactly what you should be working on at any given moment.

That proposal? The emails to respond to? The invoice to pay? Imagine if all these things had a place in your schedule, and you could go through the day confident that things were going to happen instead of trying to do them all at once.

A Weekly Work Flow is a vital tool for entrepreneurs because it is not about creating a rigid, time-blocked schedule, but rather a thoughtful approach to a scaffold you can build our schedule against. It can help you to be more productive and efficient with your time, prioritize your to-dos, and manage your energy. This way, you can get the right things done and avoid feeling overwhelmed or burned out.

Maybe each day starts with a "Set Up for the Day" block, when you check your schedule, prep dinner, and bring coffee to your desk to get started. Then you have blocks set up throughout the week to focus on content creation, client calls, responding to email, client projects, family time, and self-care.

Your Weekly Work Flow can be as flexible or as structured as makes sense for you, your business, and your lifestyle. Before we dive in, print out the Weekly Work Flow worksheet at http://focus-sessions.com/bookbonus and gather some Post-it notes and a few colored pens or highlighters.

Step 1: Know What Needs to Be Done

Brainstorm all of the things that need to be done on a weekly basis in your business and life. This includes not only your daily tasks but also your long-term goals and personal priorities. To get started, look back at past calendars and to-do lists to see what you actually have on your schedule. This information will give you a good idea of the different things that you need to get done.

Once you have completed your brainstorm, group the items into buckets of similar tasks and categories. For example, you might have buckets for client work, meetings and collaborations, content creation, marketing and visibility, learning, admin and finance, and personal time. Remember to include white space and personal self care activities like workouts, lunch, meditation, journaling, or any other activity that brings you joy and helps you recharge.

Step 2: Solidify Time Parameters

Assign an amount of time you need for each of the buckets you created in step 1. To do this, you'll need to know the total amount of expected or typical work time you have available each week. Look back to the section on setting work hours or go through your calendar and count up the time you usually spend on work.

Once you know the total amount of work time, you can assign times to each of the buckets from step 1. For example, you might want to spend eight hours a week on client work, two hours on team meetings and collaborations, five hours on marketing and so on. Write down the amount of time you want to allocate to each bucket. If the amount of time you think you should spend working is more than the amount of time you actually have on your calendar ... that's totally normal!

SIDEBAR: Time Distribution

While everyone's needs are different and everyone's business and life requires different amounts of time, here is a sample percent breakdown to get you started when it comes to thinking about how much time you want to assign to each area of your business in your week.

- 10-15% = Highest Contribution or Most Important Work
- 25% = Product creation or delivery (this is client work)
- 10% = Sales
- 10% = Marketing
- 20% = Administrative and team communication
- 15% = Buffer time
- 5% = Finances

(Note: often your Highest Contribution is around marketing and sales, so you would add those times together. If your Highest Contribution this quarter is around getting the word out about a new offer, you might spend 20% of your time– 10%+10% – on marketing)

Step 3: Create Your Weekly Work Flow Template

The last step is to create your actual workflow on your Weekly Work Flow worksheet (head to http://focus-sessions.com/bookbonus to download a blank worksheet).

First, highlight any non-negotiable "life" activities.

Use another color to block out the work hours you chose back in Chapter 10. Remember these don't have to fill all your available time!

Now, within your work times, get more specific about how you will structure your time. For example: maybe Tuesdays and Thursdays from 9-12 p.m. are content time, and Wednesdays from 10-2 p.m. are call times. Or create a guide or a "cheat sheet" that reminds you that each week you need to find time for six hours of client calls or four hours of writing.

When creating your schedule, think about when you have the most energy and focus during the week and day. Schedule your most important and demanding tasks for those times.

Grade A tasks or Highest Contribution go in your more focused time. Schedule other tasks for times when you either need less energy or the task actually gives you energy. This can be flexible or change over time. Perhaps your Highest Contribution in this season is putting your headphones on and writing, but in the next season it's all about getting out and publicly talking about what you wrote.

To create a successful Weekly Work Flow, it's important to revisit it every quarter and adjust it as needed. This will ensure that your schedule reflects your changing priorities and responsibilities in both your business and personal life.

Weekly Workflow Tips:

Tip 1: A/B Weeks

If you don't want to repeat the same Weekly Work Flow every week, you don't have to. Especially if you work a smaller number of total hours during a week, trying to fit everything you need to do for your entire business into each and every week can mean a lot of task switching, which can make focus hard to come by. Depending on your business and your work style you might prefer to create what I like to call an A/B week schedule.

In its most basic form, this might look like blocking all the things you need to do over a two-week period instead of a single week. Maybe instead of theme days, you have theme weeks. For example, perhaps an A week is a Client Week where you schedule all your client calls and other meetings, then a B week is a Content Week where you limit your calls and focus on content creation. Or perhaps in A weeks you focus on external business activities like marketing, speaking, networking, and social media, then in B weeks you focus on internal business like serving current clients and visioning the next steps in your business. If you have a creative business, maybe you have A weeks completely devoted to creating your art or in your studio, then B weeks where you handle business activities like invoicing, website updates, speaking to vendors, etc. A and B weeks can look like anything that works for your business.

A and B weeks don't have to rotate evenly either. Perhaps you block one A week a month where you completely clear your calendar and schedule big, open-ended blocks of time for batch writing, working on a new program, writing your book, or anything else that helps your business move forward. Then you spend three B weeks doing all your normal business activities, like working with clients, meeting with your team, tending to your finances, attending networking events, etc. Then you repeat the cycle the next month, with one full week devoted to creation, and three weeks devoted to running your business. (Actually, this sounds delightful, I'm off to rearrange my schedule ...)

Tip 2: Create Theme Days

Taco Tuesday anyone? Theme days are a way of setting a repeatable structure to your week without the specificity of time blocks. Theme days are deciding a set day (or time within a day) when a certain activity always happens. That means you don't have to decide when that activity is going to happen, and your brain gets used to the trigger of it happening on that day. If it's Tuesday, we're having tacos.

This works great for business tasks as well. I love my Financial Friday. (Can you tell I also love alliteration?) Knowing that I have time set aside every Friday morning to focus on reviewing my numbers, sending invoices, paying bills, and taking care of other financial tasks means I don't have to think about it at all during the week. I don't have to remember to pay a bill when it comes in, I just add it to my list for Friday. You could always create content on Thursdays or schedule all your personal appointments for Wednesdays after lunch. What you do in this time might change week to week, but you know you have time set aside for that theme's activities.

I find that setting up themes in your week takes some of the thinking off your already-full brain. Just like you don't have to think, "What's for dinner?" if you always make tacos on Tuesday, you don't have to think about when you're going to write that blog post if you always do it on Thursday. Theme days also help us set boundaries. If you set Monday and Wednesday as client call days, it's a lot easier to stick to that. Rather than going back and forth with a client to schedule a call, you can say "I have time on Monday and Wednesday next week, what is better for you?" Better yet: Send them a link to your online scheduler that only has these times available.

Turn the page for a sample Weekly Workflow, then create your own in your *Focused Workbook*.

Sample Weekly Workflow:

	Monday	Tuesday	Wednesday	Thursday	Friday	Saturday	Sunday
6:00							
7:00							
8:00	School dropoff						
	Opening Routine			Opening Routine			
9:00	Clear the Deck	Client Calls		Grade A Focus Time	Grade A Focus Time		
10:00						Kids' Soccer	
11:00			Errands & Appointments				
12:00							
1:00	Closing Routine			Closing Routine			
2:00							
	School pickup						
3:00							
4:00				Band Practice			
5:00							Family Dinner
6:00					Date Night		
7:00							
8:00							
9:00							

Your Weekly Work Flow is not a set it and forget it thing. Your schedule will change, and what you want to be focusing on will change as well. I recommend reviewing your Weekly Work Flow template every 90 days.

The Business of Focus: Cara Chace on Finding Your Flow with Theme Days

Cara Chace is a productivity and business mentor and the creator of the Theme Day Planning Method. Early in her entrepreneurial career, she found that time blocking was making her feel like a failure. She realized that, while she needed structure to be able to plan her week, she needed a system that was going to be flexible enough to allow for life's unexpected hiccups (e.g., a sick kiddo).

Cara tells us, "Theme Day Planning Method was something I came up with back in 2015 as I was reaching burnout, to take pieces of time management and productivity and make them work differently for my needs as a busy mom trying to build a business."

The basic principle of the Theme Day Planning Method is taking the list of all your to-do's and grouping similar tasks together into "theme buckets." By setting Theme Days we can avoid context switching (shifting focus and attention between tasks and/or activities), one of the biggest time and energy wasters for entrepreneurs. Theme Day Planning also enables us to set better boundaries for ourselves and others. By setting aside a Theme Day for the most important goal that you're working on each day, you will achieve that goal faster and with more ease.

Cara also suggests setting monthly Theme Days for other areas of your life like a "kiddo day," "date night," and a "hooky day."

Theme Days work because they allow you to get crystal clear on your priorities, out of overwhelm with your to-do list, and makes scheduling your week easy. Theme Days also give you enough structure with boundaries and planning, while still being flexible enough for when life happens.

You can learn more about Cara and her Theme Day Planning Method here: http://carachace.com

SIDEBAR: Changing your Schedule

If you want to make changes like these to your schedule, plan the shift well in advance. Don't try to make the change next week. You likely already have things scheduled, and trying to force existing appointments around a new system can cause frustration and make you more likely to give up. If you want to make a change, give yourself ample time to move your client calls or team meetings into an A/B schedule, or block that content creation week for six weeks out so you have a transition period and can protect that time from last-minute changes.

Plan Your Week

Weekly Work Flow, theme days, and A/B weeks are all structures that help you keep all the pieces in your week, but you also need to book time to plan exactly what you'll do with your time. I like to plan on Mondays and call these planning sessions "Momentum Mondays" (see...more alliteration), but you could plan your week at the end of the day Friday or Sunday night.

It takes about 15 minutes to go over your week's schedule, set your top priorities for the week, review your financial metrics to make sure you are on track, and plan focused time for your Most Important Work.

Remember the house you want to build? The impact you want to make? Your Highest Contribution? Declare the one specific task that moves that forward. This is your Most Important Work. If you do nothing else this week, or more realistically, if you get immersed in whatever else comes up, what is the one step you will take towards that bigger goal? What is the single most important thing you need to do this week? I call this your Momentum Focus.

Write your Momentum Focus in big, bold letters on your calendar or on a note over your desk.

Just think: If you declare a Momentum Focus each week then actually do that one thing, in a year you'll have taken 52 steps to complete your Most Important Work. That's pretty significant.

Momentum Monday morning will save you so much time (and so much stress) over the rest of your week.

Weekly Planning Process

Here is my specific 8-step process:

Analyze Last Week: Start by asking yourself: What worked last week? Notice if you were able to focus at the times you set aside. Were you able to complete your Momentum Focus tasks? What do you want to change?

Weekly Download: This is your chance to "catch" all the loose to-dos and ideas that float around all week, and especially over the weekend. Sweep last week's list, thoughts still in your brain, notes, emails, etc. all into one place. You are not creating a to-do list yet, just capturing all the ideas so you can get them out of your head and into a place where you can process them.

Set Your Schedule: Write down or review any set appointments already scheduled on your calendar. Then block your weekly work hours. Remember, just because you can work at a certain time, doesn't mean you should! Use this time to plan when you'll be working or when you'll be focused on other parts of your life.

Schedule Your Focus Sessions: Decide specifically where on your calendar you'll get your focus time and block out that time to get your Most Important Work done. Remember, you are not meant to focus all the time, so declare the day and time ahead of time when you will focus each week.

Review Big Goals: Review your quarterly goals or bigger projects in progress. What actions do you need to take this week to move these projects forward? Add those to the brainstorm you did in Step 2. Often your weekly download produces the more mundane tasks, so make sure your most important tasks have a spot in your week as well.

Top Priority: Declare your most important thing this week: your Momentum Focus. What is the single thing this week that will do one of these things:

1. Move your business forward (or impact your bottom line).
2. Get you to how you want to feel this week.

3. Make things easier for next week and clear the way for bigger projects.

Triage your task list: Ask yourself, "How can I do the most good with my available time?" Filter that Weekly Download for the most important tasks this week. What can be eliminated (from this week or altogether)? What can be delegated or what can be systematized to take less time?

I go through my download and put a "★" by the things I need to do this week, a "→" by the things that can be moved into next week, and a "**D**" (or a team member's name) by the things that I can delegate.

Schedule your tasks: Once you have blocked out your work hours, scheduled your set appointments, and blocked out your focus time, you should know how much time you have left in your week for your task list. Now that you know exactly the time you have this week, you can assign days and time to your tasks. Put tasks directly on your calendar or create daily to-do lists.

You can find a blank calendar as well as a printable bookmark with these steps at http://focus-sessions.com/bookbonus.

Making Planning Work

What if planning your week is hard? I get it! Sometimes it is hard to plan out your whole week on Monday. You might not know everything that needs to be done, or some of your schedule and tasks depend on other people. Try setting two mini sessions: one on Monday to plan the beginning of the week, and another on Wednesday to plan the rest of your week.

You might also find it helpful to do a mini version of these steps each morning. At the start of each day;

- Braindump what you need to do
- Review your set schedule and assess your available time
- Decide when you are going to focus during that day
- Choose your top priority to focus on
- Schedule the rest of your tasks or move them to another day

You may be tempted to jump straight into completing tasks so you can check them off your list, but having a set agenda for your day that ensures you're working on the right tasks will help you be more efficient and get more done overall!

CHAPTER 12:
SET UP A SCHEDULE THAT WORKS FOR YOU

FOCUS ON THIS

- Creating a Weekly Work Flow is a way to make sure all the categories of things you want to do have space on your calendar in a flexible way.
- Theme days or A/B weeks take the thinking out of planning your week and give you flexibility in their execution.
- Setting aside weekly time to plan your week will help ensure your Most Important Work and everything else has a spot on your calendar.

CHAPTER 13:

PROTECTING DISTRACTION-FREE TIME ON YOUR CALENDAR

You envision your future, you attend an inspiring talk, you set goals with your team, you read a motivating book. You get hyped up to work on a project that will really make an impact, something that will really move your business and your life forward. You know it could be a game changer. And gosh darnit, you are going to Take Action!

Then a client calls with an emergency, a kid is home from school sick, your team member moves to Bali ... life happens.

You jump in, you get things done, you do the urgent things that no one else is doing. You pick up the ball that would otherwise get dropped ... and you reschedule your Most Important Work for another day. It will calm down after you finish this launch, once the kids are back in school, or once you onboard the new team member. You tell yourself you'll get back to the game changer "once I get through this."

I hate to tell you this: You are rescheduling your future.

Those important actions, those hard things that take some courage, the work that requires you to really sink into your genius ... Those things never rise to the top of your to-do list on their own. The unpaid invoice, the urgent email reply, the viral TikTok video will somehow always beat out the most important thing ... unless you actively choose to prioritize your focus work.

You are meant to change the world. You are meant for big things. You have to make the time to DO the big world-changing things. You have to make time for the Most Important Work.

How do you make sure you have time to do your Most Important Work? **You have to block out distraction free time on your calendar and ruthlessly protect it.**

No one will block out the time for you. Your client won't say, "Email me back after you finish that sales page you're working on." Your team member won't say, "Why don't you do your important work first? My urgent question can wait." Your child won't volunteer to get their own snacks until you are done with your memoir.

You have to schedule your future.

Put it on your calendar in red permanent marker. Block that time as unavailable in your scheduler. When someone wants to schedule a meeting, don't offer that time. When the time arrives, turn off your notifications, close your office door, and put on noise-canceling headphones. Put a sign on your door and a message in Slack that says, "I am entering the zone of focus, please don't interrupt."

Protect that time at all costs.

"But Megan," I can hear you saying, "I can't find any distraction-free time!" You're not alone, read on.

How to Get Distraction-Free Time on Your Calendar

In order to get your Most Important Work done, you have to have dedicated time on your calendar to do it. Here are three ways to get your important work time on your calendar.

- **Schedule it**
- **Plan it**
- **Set it**

I used to call these three ways to get time on your calendar the good, better, and best way to set your focus time. But honestly, different techniques are going to work for different people and at different times in your life. One isn't necessarily better than the others; there is no one correct way to plan! Plan in the way that works best for you in the moment and the season you are in.

Schedule It.

Each week, or even each day, look at your calendar and block out between 30 and 90 minutes when you can focus on your Most Important Work. Look for holes in your calendar and declare time blocks when you will focus. This method is the most flexible of the options. This might work for you if your week is less structured or you're working around someone else's unpredictable schedule, like a young baby. For example, you might not be in a place to say, "I will focus at 10 a.m. on Friday," but you can plan your day to say, "When the baby goes down for her morning nap, I will focus on this most important thing while she sleeps."

The problem with this method: If you're anything like me, your week is probably already pretty scheduled. If you have open blocks of time, it might not be in your peak focus time. It might not be the length of time you want to dedicate to your Most Important Work. You might have 30 minutes here or 45 minutes there, but maybe you want to block out a longer time and really take advantage of that 90 minute sweet spot of focus time.

Plan It.

If you know you want to focus at a certain time of day or for a certain length of time, you may need to skip ahead a couple of weeks to where your calendar isn't quite as full. Then pre-schedule times that you're going to focus. Claim that time for yourself before somebody else does!

You're going to be a lot less likely to give up those times if they've been on your calendar for a while. You start to treat it as an appointment, like a client call or a dentist appointment. You're less likely to schedule something else there because it's already blocked on your calendar.

Having that time already set on your schedule also can alleviate anxiety or quiet that part of your mind that tells you to do all the things all at once. If you already have 9-10:30 next Friday blocked out to write your sales page copy, it reduces pressure to do the sales page copy today, because you know when it will get done.

This method works really well for people who have a little more control over their schedule but might struggle with setting boundaries around other people wanting their time. It also works for people who can get overwhelmed trying to figure out when all the items on their to-do lists can actually get done.

Set It.

The last way to get focus time is to create recurring appointments with yourself and your Highest Contribution. Perhaps you set every Tuesday and Thursday from 12–1:30 as focus time on your calendar. Over time it becomes a non-negotiable, and, back to our discussion of routines, your brain starts to know that if it's Tuesday at noon, it's time to focus. Other people will start to understand this time, too. Your team will know that every week you are unavailable from noon to 1:30, or your partner will know that every Wednesday evening you are unavailable to help with dinner prep if that is your scheduled focus time.

Based on these three ideas —Schedule It, Plan It, Set It—which do you think will work best for you? Look at your calendar now.

- When can you schedule some focus this week?
- Think back on your best work time based on your energy levels. Decide when an ideal focus time would be. Look ahead in your calendar and block it off the next time it is available.
- Go ahead and set that time on a regular basis.

I use a hybrid of all of these in any given week or based on what I'm currently working on. I like to have two standing Focus Sessions on my calendar each week (Set it). They are my non-negotiables, and I know that each week, I'll move my important work forward during these times.

If I am working on a specific project (like writing this book or taking a course), I'll look at my schedule for the duration of that project and plan out additional Focus Sessions for that time (Plan it). Last spring, I took a six-week writing course. The course suggested setting aside four hours a week for the material, so I blocked out three 90-minute sessions a week for that six-week time period to make sure I was able to successfully complete the course work.

Finally, when I plan my week, I schedule additional Focus Sessions as needed. While I usually already have two to three Focus Sessions on my schedule from the first two methods, I'll add in one or two more focus times that work around my schedule so that I make sure I have at least 10% of my work time set aside for my Most Important Work, and some other focus time to get planning or other tasks done.

How to Keep Focus Time on Your Calendar

You need to set and maintain boundaries to keep focus time in your days. Start by communicating that boundary to other people. This does two things:

- It sets expectations
- It creates accountability

Let others know you are entering your focus time and when you'll be available. This might mean letting your team know you won't be available for questions or telling your kids you need 20 minutes to work and they can watch one show on the iPad. Sometimes just letting others know you need some time is enough.

While working on this book, I put the following into our team Slack channel:

Megan 12:43 PM

OK all **@channel** I'm muting slack for a few hours. I'll check in before the end of my day.

By letting my team know I was going to be focusing for the afternoon, they knew I wouldn't be available and when I was going to check back in. I also paused Slack notifications to avoid the temptation of chiming in when they sent messages to each other. I enforced the boundary for others and myself.

Letting someone know that you're working also holds you accountable. My best friend and I often text each other when we're about to start working on a project, then text again to celebrate when we finish it. Just knowing that I have told someone I'm going to complete something helps me stay focused.

Each online coworking Focus Session starts with members declaring their tasks for that work period and ends with a rating on how they felt it went. No shame, just reflection to keep members accountable, even to themselves.

Research backs this up! Floyd Henry Allport, a psychologist and pioneer in the field of social psychology, conducted research on accountability and its impact on motivation and task completion. In 1920, Allport showed that a group of people working individually at the same table performed better on a whole range of tasks even though they weren't cooperating or competing. Accountability creates a sense of responsibility and obligation to follow through on a task, helps you stay motivated, and encourages you to celebrate your accomplishments, too!

Tools to Keep Your Focus Time Distraction-Free

Once you've convinced others (and yourself) that your focus time is sacred, keep it that way by preventing and eliminating distractions. Remember when I messaged my team and turned off notifications? That second part was important, too. When you sit down to focus, put your computer and phone on Do Not Disturb or airplane mode.

Set up your space for focus by clearing some blank space on your desk. (Don't use this to procrastinate. You can just move piles of things you don't need off your desk for your focus time.) Close any tabs you don't need for your task at hand. Hang a Do Not Disturb sign on your door or desk. Put on noise-canceling headphones to block out distracting sounds and to indicate that you are not available.

While there are many tools to help you stay focused and avoid distractions, here are a few of my favorites:

1. Newsfeed Eradicator or other social blocking Chrome extensions: These take willpower out of the equation

and won't let you open social media sites until a set time.

2. App settings like Pause Notifications in Slack or the "focus" setting on Apple or Android products: These let you temporarily turn off notifications for a set amount of time, without having to go back in and turn them on again.
3. Focus@will — the right blend of music can help you focus
4. A timer — let your brain know that the end is coming. Work until your timer goes off. You could use one of the many Pomodoro timers online, but your phone works just as well.

Focus Sessions As a Distraction-Free Tool

Focus Sessions are 90-minute virtual coworking sessions designed for you to get your Most Important Work done. You can schedule them each week, or weeks or months in advance, to make sure that time is blocked off in your calendar.

Focus Sessions bring together dedicated time, a distraction-free zone, and the accountability of declaring what you are working on and being (virtually) with others. Your Focus Sessions membership gets you unlimited Focus Sessions each week, all facilitated by a Focus Sessions host. It's like a gym, but for productivity. It's the most productive 90 minutes of your day. You can check them out at http://focus-sessions.com/bookbonus!

You've scheduled your focus time. Next we'll figure out what you can do with that time.

CHAPTER 13:
PROTECTING DISTRACTION-FREE TIME ON YOUR CALENDAR

FOCUS ON THIS

- Protect your distraction-free time at all costs. Block time on your calendar for this week, or a few weeks out, or even set a recurring focus appointment with yourself.
- Telling others when you plan to focus uses accountability and boundary-setting to help you achieve your goals.
- Find tools like noise-canceling headphones, timers, music, and various apps that help support your focus.

PART IV

FIND YOUR FOCUS FLOW — HOW TO FOCUS

"The more you focus on what you want, the more you'll move in the direction of getting it."

Oprah Winfrey

CHAPTER 14:

HACK YOUR BRAIN FOR FOCUS

Remember Pavlov's dog?

Ivan Pavlov was a Russian psychologist who conducted famous experiments with dogs in the late 19th century. He repeatedly rang a bell when he fed dogs, then discovered that dogs would begin to salivate at the sound because they associated the bell sound with food. This phenomenon, known as classical conditioning, demonstrated that a previously neutral stimulus — the bell — can become associated with a naturally occurring reflex, such as salivation, through repeated pairings.

People aren't that different.

Human brains get triggered by smells, sounds, or routines. Having a routine or a ritual that you follow can help your brain start a task more quickly. Other routines and rituals can keep you in flow. Creating a trigger that signals that it's time to focus is a great way to start your focus time.

You can train your brain to focus!

Put on Your "Boss Pants" — And Other Triggers.

One of my clients is a yoga and wellness teacher. She spends most of her days in flowy yoga clothes working with clients, recording meditations, and coaching on wellness. But on Fridays she dresses in her "boss-lady pants," puts on bright red lipstick, and focuses the day on getting the administrative side of her business taken care of (invoices, marketing, etc.). When she puts on that particular outfit, it triggers her brain to know that it's time to do a certain kind of work.

One of my favorite triggers is noise-canceling headphones. I often use my AirPods when I'm on a client call. But when it comes time to do Deep Work, I wear my big over-the-ear noise-canceling headphones, tune into some focus music, and my brain knows it's time to focus. (Check the resource section at http://focus-sessions.com/bookbonus for my favorite focus playlist.) Not only does my brain know that it's time to get to work, but if I'm working at home with kids around or in a place with other people (like a cafe or a coworking space) the big gray headphones also serve as a cue that I don't want to be bothered.

Perhaps when it's time to put in focus time, you light a candle. Not only does the scent help you focus, but the ritual of lighting the candle and inhaling the scent tells your brain it's time to focus on a specific project. When that focus session is over, blow out the candle to signal that your brain can relax after the more intense focus period. That keeps the ritual specific to a certain kind of work.

You can also create a trigger around a place. Maybe you do your focus work at your desk, but you take client calls or do your admin work at a table. Moving locations can be a trigger that you are switching tasks (or switching off the difficult tasks). As tempting as it is to work anywhere, it's hard to focus on your Highest Contribution from your couch, bed, or even your dining table. Sitting down at my desk triggers my brain to know it's time to start my work day. When I'm done for the day, I don't bring my laptop to the couch — this reminds my brain it's time to unwind for the day.

And if you're wondering about this science, think about Pavlov's dog again: You want to give your brain triggers so it knows what's coming next.

The Focused Mind: Concentrate on What Matters

When we were first building the beta of Focus Sessions, I knew I wanted what we were creating to be based in science and research. I knew the science of productivity and the research around time management, but I wanted to know how our brains worked to influence our ability to focus. I turned to my friend & teammate Miriam Burke, who is an expert at behavior modification and brain science to help us create the best practices for creating a focused mind, not just focus time. The following section was written with her expertise.

Keeping a focused mind is hard. There's a world of distractions waiting for you at any given time. A message, an email, a sound, a thought, an emotion, or a memory can take your attention away from your work. There seems to be a constant battle between the intention to focus and do the work, and the primal need to attend to all the distractions.

The ability to screen out distractions and focus your mind is one of the most important tools you can possess. And the good news? Not only can you learn to cultivate, grow, and control it, but you can learn to master it and concentrate on what truly matters to you.

The biggest challenge for even the most focused comes from the emotional turmoil of your life, like a recent blow-up in a close relationship that keeps intruding into your thoughts. Such thoughts barge in for a good reason: to get you to think through what to do about what's upsetting you.

The power to disengage from your feelings or thoughts and shift your attention to another is essential for well-being. Cultivating your emotional balance enables you to effectively manage emotional distractions and improve your focus.

So how do you work through distractors and get into focus?

Become aware of your emotions

Thoughts create emotions, emotions drive your actions (or inactions), and emotions can strongly impact your focus. So whenever you feel racing thoughts and emotions arise, stop everything you are doing, take a deep breath, and ask yourself, "What am I feeling right now?" The simple act of asking this question will immediately stop the emotions from rising and will allow you time to engage your rational brain.

Breathe

Intentional breath stimulates the growth of new brain cells in the cerebral cortex, the part of the brain that plays a key role in memory, attention, focus, perception, cognition, awareness, thought, language, and consciousness. By slowing down your breathing and paying attention to its rhythm, your mind becomes more focused, your emotions are soothed, and your body feels calmer and more relaxed. The good news is that breathing is always available to you. So next time you're struggling to focus, try pausing to complete some breathing exercises. (see sidebar for techniques.)

Find accountability partners

Focusing alone is hard! Humans are social creatures. When you work with others or share your experiences, you feel part of something larger than yourself. Sharing an interest draws individuals closer, even if you don't know each other, you feel connected. This feeling of connection and security calms your body, allowing the brain to process more information and make connections more broadly. This state is essential for focusing on complex thinking, decision making, creative writing, and higher-level processing. Having accountability partners will help you to show up and keep going.

Enlist a friend or two who you feel comfortable talking to about your life, work, and projects. These are friends you can bounce ideas off of; who you can share challenges, successes, and milestones with; who you can ask for feedback, and other ways of support.

Join a coworking group, physical or virtual. Simply being surrounded by people can help you get your Most Important work done.

SideBar: Breathing for Focus

Box Breathing (or 4-4-4-4 Breathing)

Inhale through your nose for a count of 4. Hold the inhale for a count of 4. Exhale for a count of 4, and hold the exhale for a count of 4. Repeat this breathing for three to four rounds.

Triangle Breathing (or 4-4-8 breathing)

Inhale for a count of 4. Hold the inhale for a count of 4. Exhale for a count of 8. Note that the exhale is longer than the inhale. Repeat this breathing for three to four rounds.

Straw Breathing

This is a powerhouse for focus. By concentrating on the exhale, you stimulate the cerebral cortex — the largest region of the cerebrum in the mammalian brain that plays a key role in memory, attention, perception, cognition, awareness, thought, language, and consciousness!

Inhale through your nose for a count of 4. Purse your lips and gently breathe the air out of your mouth very slowly, as though you are breathing out through a straw. At the same time, relax all of the muscles in your body. Exhale for a count of 8 (if 8 is too long, exhale for a count of 6). Imagine a wave of relaxation flowing down your body from the top of your head to the soles of your feet. Repeat the process for five rounds or more.

CHAPTER 14:
HACK YOUR BRAIN FOR FOCUS

FOCUS ON THIS

- The brain is capable of learning to focus. Use practice and routines to get into focus mode.
- Use triggers like a candle or noise-canceling headphones to signal to your brain that it's time to focus.
- Be aware of your emotions, thoughts, and external distractions that are competing for your attention. Use tools like breathwork to bring you back into your focus.

CHAPTER 15:

CREATE YOUR OWN FLOW FOR FOCUS

Creating a series of steps your brain goes through is one of the best ways to signal that it's time to focus. At Focus Sessions, we have developed a science-backed productivity framework to start all of our virtual coworking Focus Sessions. We call this series of steps our Focus Flow. Our Focus Flow helps our members prepare for their session, be realistic with their time, and manage their energy more effectively. It allows them to drop into a focus state quickly and to get the right things done. Feel free to create your own Focus Flow for your focus time, or borrow ours!

Prepare:
Join your Focus Session
Turn off notifications
Close extra computer tabs
Close your door or put on headphones

Arrive:
Ground yourself
Focus on your breathing
Clear your mind of stress & tension
Get calm and present

Declare:
Choose your bucket
Write your focus task on a Post-it
Stick your note where you can see it

Share:
Hold up your Post-it to the screen
Type into the chat
Say it out loud (muted or unmuted)

Prepare

The first step in our flow is to prepare for the session. You want to set yourself up for success with the fewest distractions, and with everything you'll need close at hand. Put your phone in airplane mode and turn on Do Not Disturb on your computer notifications. Close out tabs on your computer that you won't need for your focus work, especially things like email, Slack, or social media that can be a black hole of distraction. Also prepare your physical workspace: move papers off to the side, or close open files or planners. It's hard to focus on your Deep Work if an outstanding phone bill is staring back at you.

Prepare yourself physically, as well. Make sure you have water, coffee, green juice, or snacks - whatever you need to stay focused during your session. Use the restroom, shut your door, put the dog out (or let them in if you have a needy one). Think ahead to anything that might distract you from being able to focus. Nothing breaks your focus like a grumbling stomach or a full bladder.

Lastly, prepare anything you will need for your focus task. Don't waste your precious focus time looking for the file you need on your computer or waiting for a document to print. Plan and gather what you'll need to be successful ahead of time.

Arrive

You've reduced outside distractions, but your mind is probably still jumping all over the place. This step in the flow signals to your brain that it's time to shift gears and get ready to concentrate.

This is usually a short breathing exercise. This could be as simple as three deep inhales and exhales, or following the flow of your breath for a couple of minutes. Sometimes it's a body scan, listening to a focus song, or doing specific breathwork, like box breathing or triangle breathing. Refer to the sidebar on breathing exercises in the last chapter.

Declare

Choose your focus bucket (Planning, Deep Work, or Clear the Deck) and commit to the one thing you are going to focus on during your Focus Session. By declaring what you are going to work on and what bucket it fits in, you can track your overall progress and learn what works best for you. For example, perhaps you like to do a Clear the Deck session early in the day to eliminate distractions for a Deep Work session in the afternoon, or you like to plan on Monday morning and then Clear the Deck on Friday to close out the week.

Write down your focus task for the day. Research in the ADHD community has shown that writing down what you are working on and keeping it in a visible place, such as a Post-it note on the corner of your computer screen, can be an effective strategy for staying on task. Commonly referred to as a "Visual Task Reminder," it is a simple yet effective tool to stay focused and avoid getting sidetracked. If you do get distracted, the visual reminder can help cue you to get back to what you wanted to work on. By keeping the task front and center, you're better able to stay organized and complete work efficiently, leading to improved productivity and reduced stress. Additionally, the act of physically writing down the task can help to solidify the goal in your mind and increase motivation to complete it.

Share

In addition to declaring to yourself what you are working on, share it for additional connection to your task and accountability. In Focus Sessions we ask members to type their task in the chat or show their Post-it note to the group. If you are creating your own focus flow, you could tell somebody in your workspace or text a colleague, "For the next 45 minutes, I'm going to be working on a new presentation for my business."

The Importance of Community and Accountability

Dr. Laura Riordan, Transitions Coach and Focus Session advisor, taught me about the concept of collective effervescence, the idea that humans want to feel part of something larger than themselves. We are social creatures and we are shaped by the people around us.

The term collective effervescence began with 19th-century sociologist Émile Durkheim, who used it to explain what happens during religious rituals. Social psychologist Shira Gabriel, who studies collective effervescence in a broader context, describes it as the feeling of connection you get in a group experiencing the same thing, like being at a concert, sporting event, or political rally. She explains, "Even if you don't know the other members, you feel like the moment is special, something that transcends the regularness of normal life."

Collective effervescence is a prosocial emotion that attunes you to others. You feel a part of something larger than yourself and, in turn, more secure. The collective experience stimulates the vagus nerve which calms your body, allows your brain to process more information, and make connections more broadly. This state is essential for focusing on complex thinking, decision making, creative writing, and most higher-level processing. Showing up to a Focus Session helps you feel collective effervescence which, as an added bonus, Shira Gabriel has found "is strongly predictive of feeling like your life has meaning.

You can create your own focused time block, and you can get a lot out of doing it alone, but something special happens when you focus with other people. By adding in community and accountability, you amplify the work you can do alone.

Having other people present and engaged in focused tasks can boost your motivation. One study showed that the mere presence of another person improves performance by 16–32%. One of the ways to create this community support and accountability is by sharing what you are planning on working on during your focus time. This could look like simply texting a friend about your task or meeting up with a friend with the agreement that you both will put on your noise-canceling headphones and co-work next to each other. You can join a community dedicated to creating focus time, like our Focus Sessions!

You Are Ready to Start

The last part of our Focus Flow is to start. Even the first time you go through a Focus Flow, you may already feel more ready than usual to drop into your task. Remember, though, that focus takes practice. You are training your brain.

Once you commit to the above steps (Prepare, Arrive, Declare, Share), you'll likely find you can drop into a focused state more easily, and you'll build momentum to keep going. Many of our Focus Sessions members say that after attending Focus Sessions regularly, their overall focus improves and it's easier to get into a focus state. This all has to do with building momentum and strengthening your focus muscle.

Build Momentum with Gamification

I've become obsessed with this puzzle game on my phone. What keeps me coming back? How good it feels to pass each level — and game developers know this. We can look to the world of video games for some research on how to make ourselves more excited about progression and momentum.

When we win a round, our brain gets a little hit of dopamine — the feel good substance in our brain. As players, we want to feel that success again, so we are willing to keep playing. Developers know to make the wins easier and more frequent early on in the game. Early wins make us feel successful and get us excited to play the game more, even as the game gets harder. Whether you believe video games are addictive or not (the research is conflicting), there is no doubt that we like the way we feel when we win and it helps motivate us to keep going. If something is too arduous, it's much harder to be motivated to keep going.

What does this mean for focus and productivity? Here are two ways to apply these lessons.

Create early wins for yourself

The secret to early wins comes back to breaking your projects down into small, manageable tasks. Just like it would be no fun to play a game if you couldn't even pass the first level, it's not motivating to look at your to-do list and see "Launch a Podcast" day after day without ever making any progress. When you instead set a task like "Brainstorm episode ideas" or "Research the best microphones for podcasting," you start to build momentum for your project. As the tasks get harder, like pitching your first guest or figuring out a tech piece, you'll have created early wins, and the success will build your confidence to keep going.

Work in sprints

When you have a big project, like redoing your website, even if you've broken it down into appropriate tasks it's easy to get overwhelmed and struggle to get started. And remember Parkinson's Principle: the time a task takes expands to fill the time you have. If you've given yourself 90 days to redo your website, it's easy to feel like you don't need to start right away, because you have plenty of time. By turning bigger projects into micro-projects, or creating a sprint around milestones (bringing dedicated time and focus to the milestone over a short period of time), you can create more momentum with less overwhelm to move your project forward.

Working in sprints also allows you to go deeper on one project at a time rather than juggle 10 at once. You'll be able to sink in and focus faster if your brain doesn't have to sort through which of your many projects you're working on. And you'll feel a sense of accomplishment at finishing 100% of one task instead of 10% of 10 tasks, thus increasing your momentum into the next micro-project.

Focus In Action: Christina Ambubuyog

I've always liked coworking in person or going to different places like the cafe or library to work. Even though I'm used to working at home, the change of environments fueled my creativity, but during the pandemic, that pretty much stopped. It's been difficult to get in a good rhythm with my work.

A lot of times I come into the Focus Session reluctantly, as if it's something that I could do myself without the support, but I show up anyways and turn on the camera and something inside of me says go time. I've learned to be okay with showing up even if I'm in resistance, trusting that I'll either get in a flow or get something done even if it's a small task.

I think simply knowing everyone is there to focus and move the needle forward in their lives and business in some way makes a difference. It's so much more fun and motivating to work together than doing things on my own.

FOCUS AFFIRMATION

PREPARE
ARRIVE
DECLARE
focus

CHAPTER 15:
CREATE YOUR OWN FLOW FOR FOCUS

FOCUS ON THIS

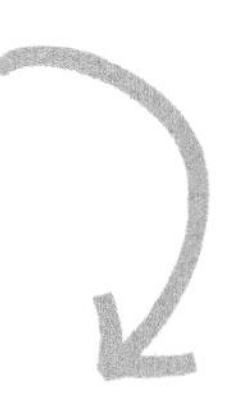

- Creating a focus flow is a great way to trigger your brain to focus.
- The steps of our focus flow: Prepare, Arrive, Declare, and Share.
- Three ways to drop into focus faster: Use community, create early wins, and work in sprints.

CHAPTER 16:

CELEBRATE, ADJUST, AND BUILD ON YOUR MOMENTUM

When your focus time is over, your Focus Flow isn't quite done. Include a practice of checking in on how your session went, so you can celebrate and learn from your experience. Remember: You are not expected to know how to focus; this is a skill you need to learn and practice over and over again. Just like a professional athlete watches video of their game, you should spend time reviewing your focus time for what works, and ways to improve the next time.

Rank and Adjust

At the end of your focus time, ask: How focused did I feel during this session? Did I accomplish what I wanted to do? On a scale of 1-5, give yourself a focus score: 5 means you felt super focused, 1 not so much for this session. Then, if you felt you had a 5 level of focus, think about what worked. Did having your task planned out help you stay focused? Did meditation before you started clear your head for Deep Work? Take note of what helped you so you can repeat it in your next focus time block.

If you felt unfocused or didn't accomplish your task, what got in the way? Were you overly ambitious about what you could get done in the time you'd allotted? Unclear on what you planned to do? Were you preoccupied with somebody else's project? Did hunger distract you? That information helps you prepare for next time.

Focus is a learned skill; you are not "good" or "bad" at focusing, you haven't yet learned all the ways to work within your unique personal system. Analyzing your focus time helps you know what worked and what got in your way. You can even write a reminder for yourself: For my next focus time, I will ______. Fill in the blank with something that worked for you or a strategy around how to avoid distractions.

Celebrate Your Wins

If you're like the hundreds of entrepreneurs I've worked with, I know you're motivated, driven, and full of amazing ideas, but you can also be hard on yourself. You think you aren't working hard enough, getting enough done, or doing a good enough job at anything.

I also know that is not true.

How often do you take time to celebrate your accomplishments? You likely complete a project, then immediately move onto the next one, because you're busy or want to jump on the next new idea. It's not common to stop to analyze where you've been, what has worked, or even just pat yourself on the back for a job well done. Focus Culture celebrates wins ... and that pays off.

When asked to evaluate progress, most people focus on what's left on a to-do list instead of what's completed. You probably don't take enough time to celebrate —or even acknowledge! — your accomplishments. Celebrating your achievements not only makes you feel good, but your wins also hold important data about what to do next.

Make sure you celebrate what you accomplished at the end of each focus session. No matter if your focus level was a 1 or a 5, you showed up for yourself and you're further along than before you started. Instead of saying, "I didn't get enough done," celebrate what you did accomplish. Your wins help you create a Recipe for Success to discover what will help you succeed next time.

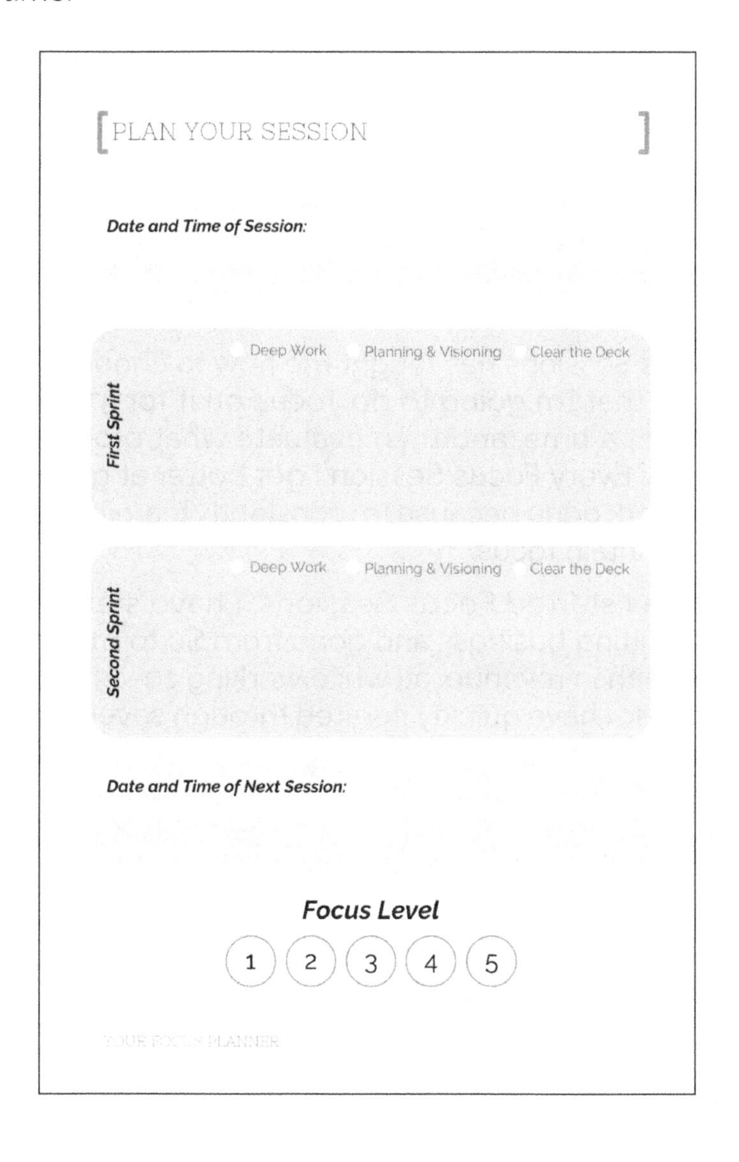

Focus In Action: Mary Frances Pickett, CPA

I only work 2.5 hours each day. Before Focus Sessions, I often napped through my work session. If I made it to my desk I would sit and spin my mental wheels because starting a new business was so overwhelming. Once I heard about Focus Sessions, I restructured my day so that my work time always matched up with a Focus Session. Now, I show up at my desk for my daily Focus Session whether I feel like it or not. Then I do some sort of focused work because the session leaders tell me to pick a task. I'm really good at doing what I'm told!

Focus Sessions has taught me how to choose the work that I'm going to do, focus on it for 37 minutes at a time, and then evaluate what broke my focus. Every Focus Session I get better at getting my work done because I'm constantly learning how to maintain focus.

Since I started Focus Sessions, I have started a consulting business and gone from $0 to $10,000 a month in revenue, all while working 10–15 hours a week. I have quickly iterated through several different offers as I figured out what type of work I can best do in a limited amount of time. Next quarter, I'll be using my Focus Sessions to write a book and build out an online course based on the 1:1 coaching that I'm doing.

Learn more about Mary Frances and her consulting business: http://profit-plan.com.

CHAPTER 16:
CELEBRATE, ADJUST, AND BUILD ON YOUR MOMENTUM

FOCUS ON THIS

- At the end of your focus time, rank your focus and use that data to help improve your focus for the next time.
- Productivity and focus are not the same thing. Prioritize focus and productivity will follow.
- Celebrate your wins and accomplishments. Use them as a tool for plotting your overall future success.

PART V

WHEN FOCUS GETS TOUGH, RAISE YOUR RESILIENCE

"You may encounter many defeats, but you must not be defeated. In fact, it may be necessary to encounter the defeats, so you can know who you are, what you can rise from, how you can still come out of it."

Maya Angelou

CHAPTER 17:

WHEN THERE IS JUST TOO MUCH TO DO

By now, you're ready to kick Hustle Culture to the curb. You're a unique individual with unique rhythms and strengths to make the impact you want to make. You know you have exactly the time you need, you've learned how to get focus time on your calendar, and you know how to create a well crafted to-do list.

But Hustle Culture is pervasive; you've been steeped in it your whole life. Remember that kitten poster in the back of your kindergarten classroom that said "Hang in There"? What that poor kitty needed was permission to take a break! So yes, you've been getting subtle messages of capitalism and Hustle Culture from the start.

When things pile up or don't go as planned, you may forget that you're an awesome Focus Culture inhabitant, and fall back into overwhelm and frustration.

No matter how much you embrace Focus Culture, sometimes you just have too much to do, too many choices, or too many other people influencing your actions and reactions. That's ok. Let's talk about it.

Let's revisit our soup one more time. Sometimes you just have too many ingredients. You feel the pressure to use them all before they go bad. Sometimes there's just too much to do and not enough time. What then?

Stop Juggling and Start Spinning Plates

You know the phrase "too many balls in the air"? It creates a visual that's easy to picture. A juggler at the circus is trying to keep all of the balls in the air at the same time. They have to rhythmically touch each ball and keep their eyes on all of the balls at the same time. If they need to add or subtract a ball to their juggling act, there's a good chance all of the balls will come crashing to the ground.

You don't want to be a juggler when it comes to the important tasks in your life.

Let's think of another circus performer, the plate spinner. The plate spinner still has to balance a lot of plates, each on a little pointed stick ... but unlike the juggler, this performer can put energy and focus into spinning one plate at a time. Once a plate has energy of its own, it can spin by itself while the plate spinner moves on to put energy into spinning another plate. If one of the plates begins to slow down the performer can go back and add some energy to that plate until it's spinning again on its own. If at any moment there are too many plates spinning, the performer can simply remove one of the plates and set it down on the table without the whole operation crashing down.

When you are feeling overwhelmed, it's easy to feel like the juggler. Instead of feeling like you have to juggle all of the tasks, think about being a plate spinner. Focus on putting energy (i.e., attention and effort) into one task at a time. Spend the morning spinning your CEO plate, then the afternoon spinning the client plate. Then those plates will spin on their own while you spin the self-care plate, the family plate, or the friends plate, knowing that tomorrow you can come back and re-energize any plates that have slowed down ... or remove any that you don't need right now.

Be Like Bamboo

Did you know that bamboo is considered one of the strongest building materials? It's stronger than oak and even steel. It gets stronger when under stress and is extremely flexible. Houses made of bamboo have been known to withstand 9.0 earthquakes (that's a big one for all you non-Californians).

Why am I talking about bamboo?

Here's the thing: Part of the reason bamboo is strong is because it's flexible. During an earthquake, the bamboo house flexes to dissipate the energy as opposed to being rigid and crumbling under the pressure.

You want your business, your plans, and frankly your life, to be strong AND flexible: to be built on a strong foundation but able to flex under pressure when the environment changes.

The Nimble Planning System is designed to give you this flexibility without needing to scrap your entire plan (or your entire business) when things change.

And not only global pandemic kind of change. What if you're presented with a great opportunity, or you want to take parental leave, or you have a brand new idea you want to launch in your business, or a family member is ill and needs more support? With the Nimble Planning System, you can adapt while still moving towards your big business goals. You can adjust your daily tasks, monthly projects, or even your goals, without losing sight of the impact you want to make and your overall purpose.

Maybe you know your impact is to help parents live more sustainably, and a goal this quarter is to expand your audience. Maybe you decide the podcast you want to start has too many to-dos for right now. Shifting your project to being a guest on other people's podcasts can help you reach your same goal, but with a less time-intensive project.

It's easier to stay out of overwhelm when you feel like you could adapt your plan instead of starting over because something changed. At the end of the quarter you can still say you accomplished your goal of spreading the word about sustainable parenting, you just accomplished it in a different way

EASY Method

Even when you've followed this system — blocked out time for the most important things and gotten really clear on your goals, projects and tasks — sometimes there is still too much to do.

I have an EASY acronym to help you thin down your obligations and get out of overwhelm..

Eliminate

Scan your to-do list, project, or calendar for tasks you can outright eliminate. How many are "must do" and how many are "should do" or even "would be nice if I have time to do"? Are there tasks that are no longer relevant? At the very least, can anything be eliminated from "right now" and rescheduled to another day, month, or even quarter? Projects can always have a version 2.0!

Automate and Delegate

This step is all about getting a person or tool to do a task for you. What on your list can be delegated to someone on your team or hired out on a project basis,? Whether they are business tasks (having your VA set up your newsletter) or home/ personal tasks (having your partner in charge of dinner or kids folding laundry), there are definitely things on your list that you do not have to do.

Can something be systematized so it takes less time? Can a piece of technology automate that email or set the crockpot for dinner? Get ruthless on what you automate and delegate — your genius is probably not in scheduling emails or sorting clothes. (Note that automating and systematizing takes some time in the setup, but it pays off again and again in the long run. Block off some focus time for setting up systems, so that the plates can spin themselves without requiring constant attention.)

Simplify and Schedule

Once the tasks have been narrowed down, ask yourself if you can simplify any of the steps. Does it all need to be included in this version? Is there an easier way to do it?

Once you do that, you can schedule any remaining tasks onto your calendar, so you know exactly when they are going to get done. This helps make sure you are being realistic as well. If you block time for tasks in your calendar, you'll be forced to think about how much can fit in each time slot. This also helps you set aside distraction-free focus time to do these most important tasks.

You are the CEO

The last step is to remember WHY you are doing each of these other steps. You are the CEO. When you choose to delegate setting up your social media, it means you get to focus on sales. If you schedule time to work on your product, you can focus on your family when it's done.

The EASY Chart

Find a printable version in your *Focused Workbook.*

Task	***Eliminate***	***Automate***		***Schedule***	***You Are the CEO***
		Systematize	Delegate		

SideBar: About Delegation

You can do anything, but you can't do everything.

I think many entrepreneurs try to disprove this statement, but in order to make the impact you want to make, you have to be able to delegate.

Delegation can be hard. Some fear giving up influence over the outcome, or compromising standards. Some worry about time and energy spent fixing mistakes. Others may fear that by delegating they will appear less competent or valuable. Delegation can be hard for people who have a strong attachment to their work (like most entrepreneurs I know!).

Delegation is essential, though. It frees up your time and resources, and helps keep you out of overwhelm and burnout.

If you are unsure what to delegate, think about where your Highest Contribution is being made. You can delegate within your business or at home to free up time, energy and mental load. You write the powerful personal story for an email to your audience, then a Virtual Assistant sets up and schedules the email. Or you define the parameters of a project and your admin sets it up in Asana and tracks that things are getting done. You can have someone write your social media posts so you can focus on sales calls or have someone do your laundry so you can focus on quality time with your kids. These are all forms of delegation that make sure you protect time to do your Most Important Work.

The Business of Focus: Meg Casebolt on Doing Less Better with Marketing Efforts

Meg is the CEO of Love At First Search, where she helps online-businesses with Search Engine Optimization (SEO). She is also the host of the Social Slowdown podcast, which is all about finding ways to market your business without being dependent on social media. She encourages us to market our businesses in a more strategic, focused way so that potential clients can discover us easily.

Meg explains that social-media marketing is built to expire, like a hamster wheel that you have to stay on all the time. Instead, she wants us to use our time creating marketing content that will go the distance and outlive the few hour lifespan of a social media post, so we can spend less time marketing and more time actually serving our clients.

The secret is to create focused, search-friendly content on channels that reward you for high quality and have a long term impact, like Google, YouTube, and podcasts. By focusing on creating content that can be discovered on these powerful search engines, you can create content that will last for months or years, not just hours.

You can learn more about Meg and SEO strategy here: http://loveatfirstsearch.com

CHAPTER 17:
WHEN THERE IS JUST TOO MUCH TO DO

FOCUS ON THIS

- Sometimes there is a lot to do! When you have a lot to focus on, think about being a plate spinner and put energy into one task at a time.
- Bamboo is strong because it's flexible. Your work and plan will be stronger if you build in both structure and flexibility.
- Look for ways to minimize your task list using the EASY acronym: Eliminate, Automate, Schedule and You are the CEO.

CHAPTER 18:

WHEN THERE ARE TOO MANY CHOICES

Picture me standing and staring in front of the fridge, unable to decide what's for dinner. Even "we could get takeout" couldn't help, because there's the burrito place,the other Mexican place we like, Thai, pizza, or the salad place .... After a day of choosing a cover for this book (I like options!) and a new tech package for my business and what to have for lunch and if I should join a new gym ... decision fatigue had set in.

Decision fatigue is the deteriorating quality of decisions made by an individual after a long session of decision making.

Sound familiar?

Decision fatigue occurs due to the mental exhaustion from having to make too many decisions. This fatigue can actually lead people to avoid making decisions entirely, a phenomenon called "decision avoidance."

We are constantly faced with a million decisions, and after three years of a global pandemic that upended systems and repeatedly put us in brand new situations, it's no surprise many of us are suffering from decision fatigue or decision avoidance. It's hard to make all the decisions and trust our decision-making ability.

Decision fatigue is a real psychological phenomena that has been researched and studied. The good news is that by recognizing it as decision fatigue — not just flakiness — we can do something about it.

Four Ways to Combat Decision Fatigue

1. Identify your best decision-making time

Studies show that people make better decisions earlier in the day, so that's a great time to plan business brainstorm sessions or calls with your team. Maybe save a potentially heated or decision-laden conversion with your spouse for a weekend, instead of getting into it after your kids are in bed for the night when you've used up your decision budget for the day.

2. Make a list of the decisions you have to make

At this point in the book, are you even surprised I'm suggesting another list? But keeping all the decisions you have to make in your head leads to overwhelm and, often, decision paralysis. So make a list. Getting your choices out of your head and onto paper helps you look at them a little more objectively. When you can see them all in front of you, you may realize that some decisions are actually easy to make and you can save the others for when you are at your decision-making peak time.

3. Reduce the number of decisions you have to make

You've probably heard that President Obama wore only gray or blue suits. He is quoted saying, "I don't want to make decisions about what I'm eating or wearing, because I have too many other decisions to make." Pre-setting some decisions is one way to avoid decision fatigue. Meal planning, writing a week's worth of social media, or getting organized for your work week on Sunday all reduce decision making fatigue during the week. If you aren't thinking about what you are wearing, eating, or posting on Instagram, you can focus on making a decision about the bigger direction of your company.

4. Get support

Two heads are better than one. If you are feeling overwhelmed or paralyzed with what the right next step is for you in your business or how you will adapt to a change that has come up in your world, seek help. Schedule a walk with a trusted friend, book a call with a business coach, or set up an appointment with a therapist. There are just too many decisions to hold in a single brain!

Above all, **trust that you make good decisions.** You are smart, pragmatic, and you have made a million good decisions in the past for your business, for your family, and for your community. Trust that you will again ... but maybe wait until tomorrow morning.

Don't Overthink It

I have been told once or twice that I can overthink things. I think it comes from being a planner. I like to go through all of the scenarios or play out different ideas in my head, but there is a point where thinking and planning extend to overthinking, and that can be counterproductive and even anxiety-producing.

First, let me define overthinking: an idea or a decision you need to make, that you continue to circle around. It can show up as getting hung up on a small piece of the decisions like – "should this program be three weeks or five weeks?"; as an insecurity or doubt – "does anyone even want this opt in?"; or even questioning everything about your life – "will this even help people?"

If you find yourself stuck in an endless loop of "what the heck should I do?" try these steps.

5. **Take a break.** Walk away, get some fresh air, switch projects. Eat, drink some water, rest. Your brain might need to reboot for you to be clear on the solution. Remember, we are not designed to focus all the time and making decisions takes focus!

6. **Write out the decision you need to make.** Your brain is not a hospitable place to hold all of your ideas. Writing out exactly what decision you are trying to make can give you some clarity. You probably are more clear on parts of your overthinking than you think; there may only be one or two decisions you need to make.

7. **Come back to your why.** What is the purpose of the project? What is the desired impact? What is the result you want? Coming back to the "why" of the decision can point you in the right direction.

8. **Address the "what if's...?"** Identify the things that are holding you back, then ask yourself if your fear is true. If it is true, what will you do then? "What if no one wants this opt-in I've created?" Then you'll create something new. "What if three weeks is too short?" You can add bonus weeks or extend it the next time.

9. **Clarity comes from action.** Sometimes we get stuck because we're afraid to make a mistake, but we learn from taking action. Can you run a beta and get more information to fine-tune? Is this the first draft? Can you make a "for now" decision and change it in the next round if you don't like it? Can this whole decision be saved for version 2.0 after you have put version 1.0 out into the world?

10. **Ask for an opinion from a trusted source.** Notice this is not the first step. You have to do the leg work in the first steps so the person you ask can see the real decision you are trying to make, not the whole contents of your head vomited out for them. You can approach a friend and ask, "I'm doing this thing. I want the results to be this, and I know I want to do this, and this, but I'm struggling with this one decision, can you help me think it through?" Sometimes

simply articulating it for somebody else helps you see it more clearly. Other times, a second opinion will help you see the options with fresh eyes or less emotion, so that you can answer that last question and move on.

Focus on Making the Next Right Decision

When people get overwhelmed, they tend to fall into two categories: freezers or tornado-ers. Freezers go deer-in-the-headlights with decision paralysis. They stare at their to-do list or their calendar. They can feel the anxiety rising, but they can't take action. There is just too much; it's just too overwhelming.

Tornado-ers start doing all the things: sending the email, rearranging the furniture, buying a new course, cleaning out the fridge. They aren't sure what to do, so they do everything. Busy must mean productive.

Even though these two types of people seem widely different in the way they approach overwhelm, the solution is actually the same.

Take one step.

Whether you respond to anxiety by staring blankly at your screen or sorting your sock drawer, the answer is the same: Make the next right decision.

You don't have to know how it will all play out, you don't have to know what step 47 is or what will happen as a result of today. Take one step. (Still feeling stuck here? Go back to Don't Overthink It.)

Ask yourself, "What is the next right decision?" and then take action!

We've made a handy flow chart to help you decide what to do. Find a larger copy inside your *Focused Workbook* at http://focus-sessions.com/bookbonus.

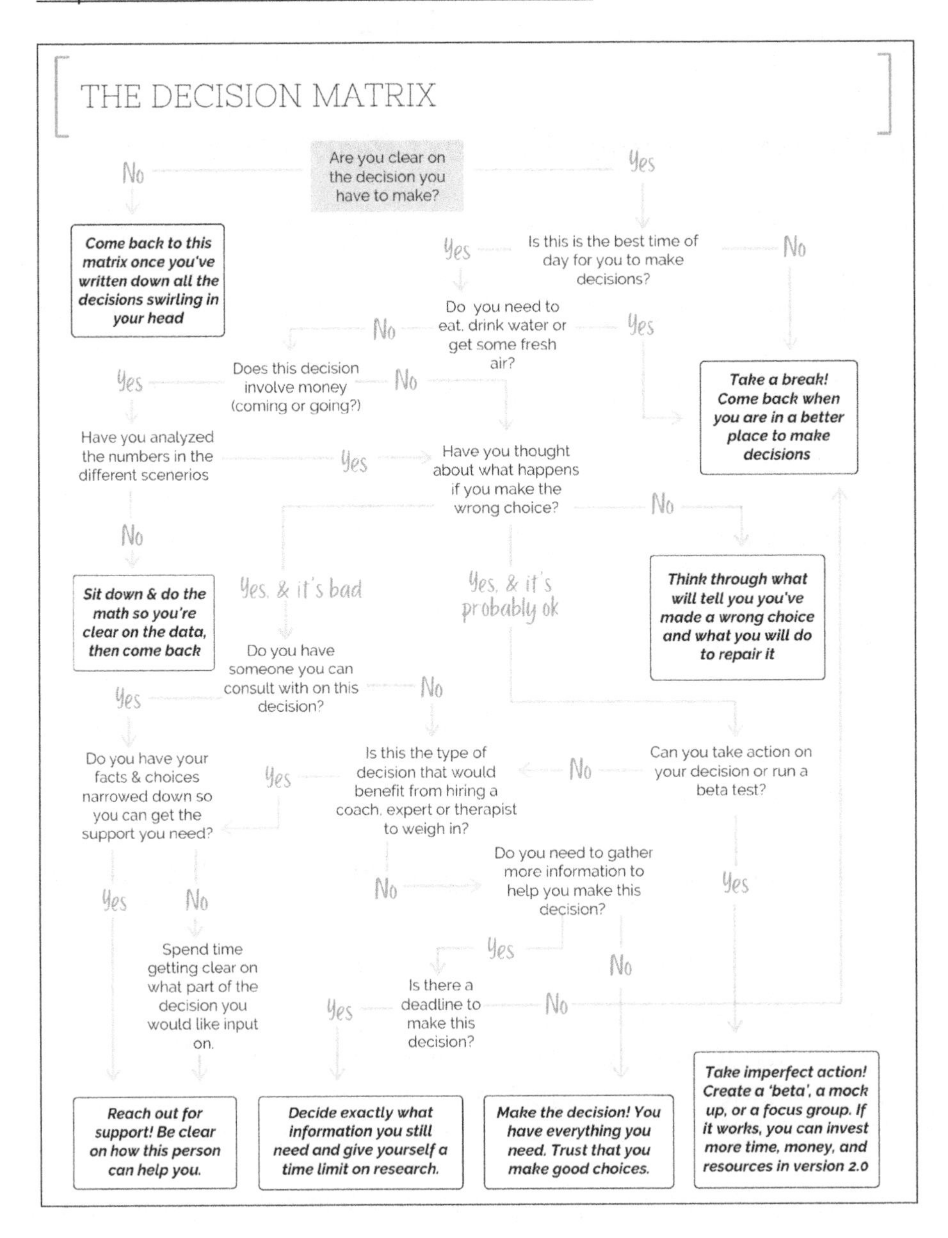

CHAPTER 18:
WHEN THERE ARE TOO MANY CHOICES

FOCUS ON THIS

- Decision fatigue is real! Look for ways you can automate or streamline some of the decisions you have to make on a regular basis.
- If you find yourself in a loop of overthinking the decisions that you need to make, try taking a break, getting clear on your why, and remember clarity often comes from action.
- When you get overwhelmed, focus on making only the next decision. Take just the next step.

CHAPTER 19:

WHEN OTHERS DISRUPT YOUR FLOW

Sometimes we have everything in place to focus when something or someone else changes that plan. Often the best laid plans are interrupted by situations beyond our control. In fact while writing this section, the power went off in my office building! None of us live in a vacuum, we have others who depend on us, and we want to be part of our communities. While we've established the importance of flexibility, it's also important for us to put measures in place to make sure we stay in charge of our days.

Others' Demands – Boundaries and Saying No

Sticking to your focus plan often involves enforcing a boundary. Whether the demand for attention is from your clients, your kids, or your team, finding a balance between meeting the needs of others while still setting time limits and boundaries for yourself is challenging. Let's look at a few strategies to help you protect your time.

1. **Remember (and Prioritize) Your Own Goals.** Everything you say "yes" to is a "no" to something else.When we say yes to someone else's requests, we are often swapping out the time that we would spend working towards our own goals and Highest Contribution. Before responding to any requests, prioritize your own goals and objectives. Ask yourself what you need to accomplish first for your own Highest Contribution and how much time this will realistically take. This will allow you to plan out your schedule and set boundaries accordingly.

2. **Communicate Clearly.** Don't be afraid to communicate your limits and expectations. This could mean stating your availability (and when you are not available) or identifying what part of their request you can do. For example, you can tell someone you'll need to leave the volunteer event at 2 p.m., not 5 p.m. as requested.

   One of my client's team members wanted to book meetings with her before starting a project. While it sounded reasonable, my client found that the teammate was using these meetings to do her own brainstorming and the meetings took more time than necessary. She asked the team member to provide a first draft of a project plan before they met, then they scheduled 15 minutes to review it.

3. **Schedule Buffer Time.** When possible, try to build buffer time into your schedule. This will give you the flexibility to take on additional requests if needed, but not at the sacrifice of working on your Highest Contribution — or even being able to take a break!

4. **Put Your Boundaries in Writing.** An easy way to help stick to your own boundaries is to write them down in a place others can easily see them. That way you don't feel like you are having to say no to people, but rather that the boundary is already in place by some "outside" force (even if that outside force is you!). For example, put your office hours in the signature line of your email.

If you write that you are in the office M–Th, 9 a.m.–2 p.m., you won't feel as pressured to reply to an email on a Saturday or even 4 p.m. If your client agreement says you meet with clients Tuesday and Thursday between 10 a.m. and 2 p.m., your clients won't expect you to meet Friday at 8 a.m. If you let your team know you will reply to Slack messages between 10-11 a.m. and 4-5 p.m. each day, they will know not to expect a reply from you at 2 p.m.

5. **Know When to Say No.** There will come a point where tasks or requests will become too much. When this happens, don't be afraid to say no. This doesn't have to be a permanent solution, but it allows you to get some much-needed breathing room to tackle the other important tasks at hand.

Deciding ahead of time how much you are willing to do for your kids' school, for your clients, or for a volunteer organization is a really helpful way to make an agreement with yourself before others ask for your time. This goes back to our idea of "make decisions once." Recently a client who volunteers extensively in her community decided that she would limit herself to four hours a week. One week, she hit that number on Monday. When someone asked if she could come back later in the week, it was easier for her to say, "I've already hit my allotted time for this week, but I'll see you next week!"

Say "No" Phrases

It can be challenging to set boundaries and say no, especially when people are counting on you for support in your personal and professional life, but sometimes we default to saying yes to things because we can't think of a polite way to say no in the moment. You may fall into that trap of thinking that because you have a flexible schedule as an entrepreneur, that you "should" be able to fit in that request. This desire to be accommodating can lead to overcommitting.

One effective way to protect your time is to have a set of "say no" phrases that you can use when you need to decline a request. Having these phrases prepared in advance can make it easier to decline in a polite manner, without feeling guilty or stressed. I recommend creating these ahead of time and even writing them down so you can pull them up when you need to say "no." Here are a few examples:

- Thank you for thinking of me, but I won't be able to take on any more commitments at this time.
- I've reached my predetermined limit on the time I can commit to that, but I'll let you know when I have more time.
- I appreciate the offer, but I have to decline.
- I'm sorry, but I have other commitments that I need to prioritize right now.
- I would love to help, but I can't fit it into my schedule.
- I can't help with that, but I'd love to recommend someone who can.
- I can't meet at that time, but I'd be happy to meet after 1 p.m. on Thursday.
- I can't organize the event, but I can ___.
- I won't be able to meet, but could you record a video or send me a voice memo of your ideas and I'll reply later?
- No. (Yes, this is a complete answer! You don't need to justify your time limitations or priorities to anyone if you don't want to.)

By having these phrases ready to use, you can effectively decline requests without feeling like you're letting anyone down. It's okay to prioritize your own work and your well-being.

SideBar: "Unlimited" Offers

Be cautious of offering "unlimited" of anything as part of your business offer, like unlimited Slack, Voxer, email access, or even unlimited access to material.

While it sounds like a great value add, without a clear boundary it can be hard for you as the provider and for the client, as well.

When you offer something that is unlimited you have to hold mental space for that offer all the time.

And what if you change the offer? Are you still beholden to the original promise?

It is much more clear cut to offer "weekly check-ins for six weeks" or "two weeks of Voxer access" or "access to the material for one year."

Not only does this allow you to budget your time and energy to serve these clients, it also gives a clear roadmap of how to work with your offer. They'll be more likely to complete the course work (and therefore get the results they want), if they know they can only check in for six weeks. Or they'll take action on that coaching call if they know that they only have two weeks to ask questions, and they won't have an unfinished course looming over their head five years from now if they lose access after 12 months.

You are in charge of your day. You get to decide how you spend your time. When you know how to say no and protect your boundaries, you put yourself back in charge of your day. You are better able to focus on your Highest Contribution and stay out of overwhelm and burnout when you are clear and realistic about what you can do.

CHAPTER 19:
WHEN OTHERS DISRUPT YOUR FLOW

FOCUS ON THIS

- When you get overwhelmed, focus on making only the next decision. Take just the next step. Boundaries are an important tool for focus. By enforcing a boundary, you are prioritizing your own goal and ultimately the impact you want to make.
- Plan ahead what your limits on your time are and create some "say no" phrases so you can decline offers to protect your time without guilt.
- Boundaries are easier to enforce when you communicate them clearly, build buffer time into your day, and know when you need to say no.

CHAPTER 20:

WHEN YOU ARE JUST OVERWHELMED

I live in Northern California, which is prone to wildfires, and part of our emergency preparedness strategy is to list the items that you would need to grab if you had to evacuate your home quickly, things that you might forget if you were in a state of shock or panic. I knew that if I were flustered trying to get my family to safety I might not think to grab my laptop, the passports, or even my purse. Now my family has a packing list in case of a fire to ensure that even if my brain were not fully functioning, I could run down my list and make sure everyone and everything gets to safety.

Create Your Own Get Out of Overwhelm Kit

Experts all agree that the best way to survive a natural disaster is to be prepared for it to happen. Like we store extra water and stock up on flashlight batteries, we can prepare for when overwhelm strikes, too. You can keep it in the Note section on your phone or on an index card on your desk.

When you are not currently overwhelmed, start by making a list of your common stress or overwhelm triggers. Maybe you get overwhelmed when there are too many things happening at once or when you're not clear on the calendar or when money is tight. Identifying these things ahead of time will help you acknowledge that something triggered your overwhelm.

Identify triggers

My triggers when I'm overwhelmed:

- Money is tight or I have a big expense
- Too many things happening at once
- Not knowing what needs to be done
- Feeling like I'm not in control
- Too many decisions to make
- Doing things I don't really want to do
- Unexpected changes
- Calendar is too full
- Lack of support

In addition, jot down signs that you are overwhelmed: Trouble sleeping, distraction, snapping at your loved ones, or even tears are all indicators that you need to use your Get Out of Overwhelm toolkit.

Identify signs of overwhelm

Signs I'm overwhelmed:

- Can't sleep
- Snapping at kids
- Procrastination
- Crying
- Avoiding work or other projects
- Too much time on social media, or any other distraction (even 'healthy' things like reading, cooking, exercise, if you are using it to avoid other responsibilities)

Once you know your signs of overwhelm and what often causes it, think of ways that usually work to get you out of it.

Identify ways out of overwhelm

What usually gets me out of overwhelm?

- Make one decision
- Talk to a friend
- Get into nature
- Workout
- Do a big braindump
- Delegate
- Make a plan
- Ask for help
- Get some sleep
- Decide what doesn't need to be done
- Reconnect with my why
- Take one step

Of course these are not the only things. Maybe dancing it out or journaling works for you. Maybe you need to clear some physical space. A Clear the Deck Session to get rid of a bunch of little tasks or tie up loose ends might feel good. You know what makes you feel better.

Sometimes when we are overwhelmed and somebody asks what they can do to help, we have no idea how to answer. Take a minute to make a list of general things that people can do to help you when you are overwhelmed: pick up dinner, put the kids to bed, run errands, remind you to drink water or eat ... If you did the work of breaking down what you have to do into small tasks, seeing your planning Post-its can remind you of tasks that are easier for you to hand off.

Overwhelm can be isolating. You feel like everyone else has it figured out, which can lead to more feelings of discouragement and overwhelm. Make a list of your go-to people. These are the people you can reach out to, to help you problem solve, give you support, or just let you vent.

Create an advisory board

- Person who I can delegate to
    - Home
    - Business
- Business colleague or friend who "gets it"
- Friend I can vent to
- Someone who helps me solve problems
- Someone who makes me laugh
- Other go to people

Next create your own Get Out of Overwhelm cheat sheet. This is like my list of what to pack in case of fire. When you are overwhelmed, your brain might be too tired to create a list of your support people or what you can do, but if you already have it done, you can look at your existing list.

Steps to Get Out of Overwhelm

1. Stop what you are doing and ________________ (get outside/hydrate/stretch/etc.)
2. Ask yourself:
    - What is my "Big Why"?
    - Why is this hard?
    - Why does this need to happen?
    - What else is going on in my life that might be showing up as overwhelm?
    - What is one thing I'm in control of?

3. Ask for help by ________ from __________
4. What boundary needs to be reestablished?
5. What do I need as a person?

Overwhelm is uncomfortable. Embracing Focus Culture, learning to do less better, and letting the impact you want to make guide you can help you stay out of overwhelm. Planning your projects and using focus time to go deep on one thing can help, too. Finally, having a plan to deal with it can help you get out of overwhelm more quickly and with more ease.

Mental Health Check-In: Not all problems can be solved with a list and a good friend. If you are experiencing extreme overwhelm, anxiety, depressive, or suicidal thoughts, please seek professional help. The most important thing is that you are healthy and sometimes we need more help than an index card to get there.

U.S. National Suicide Help Line is: 1-800-273-TALK.

A list of resources in other countries can be found at http://findahelpline.com)

FOCUS AFFIRMATION

you've
GOT THIS!

CHAPTER 20:
WHEN YOU ARE JUST OVERWHELMED

FOCUS ON THIS

- Be prepared for when overwhelm strikes. Create a list you can refer to when you're feeling anxious or stressed.
- Identify what usually triggers overwhelm and signs that you are overwhelmed.
- Create a list of tools, tricks, and people that help you move past overwhelm.

THE WORLD NEEDS YOUR MOST IMPORTANT WORK

Remember that productivity is not about getting more done, but about getting the right things done. The right things are the things that help you build the house you want to live in, make the impact you want to make, and nurture all of the parts of your life.

Productivity is a by-product of focus, and focus is a skill you can improve, not something you are inherently good or bad at.

The next time you find yourself saying, "I'm not productive, I need to focus harder" or "I'm bad at time management" or "I need more focus," turn to the skills in this book.

If you need help setting aside dedicated focus time, join us for a Focus Session. You can learn more about our membership and join us for 90 minutes of dedicated focus time, plus connect with a community of Focus Finders at http://focus-sessions.com.

The world needs your Most Important Work. Get clear on what that is. Plan out how to do it. Schedule the time to focus on deep work.

Stay focused. Let's make it happen!

ACKNOWLEDGEMENTS

This book would not be possible without the love, support, and hard work of so many people.

Sara Barry, this book would literally not have happened without your support, encouragement, writing talent, and your ability to talk me through overwhelm and out of imposter syndrome more than once. You have been a part of my business and life for more years than I can count at this point. You are my rock and my secret weapon. Thank you.

Miriam Burke, I wish every team could be as lucky to have someone like you at the helm, and every person could have a friend as special as you. Thank you for believing in me and my vision, often more than I do. You have taught me so much.

Natalie DeGoey, everything you create makes me gasp. Thank you for making this book beautiful and for your constant willingness to just make it work. And thank you for being an honest and transparent representation of so many of the topics from this book.

Meg Casebolt and Stacy Spensley, every writer needs friends who are as equally willing to edit your nonfiction book as they are to talk about dragon smut. You two give the best advice, hold me accountable, and cheer me on...often all done with Schitt's Creek GIFs. Your collective contribution to the completion of this book was nothing short of incredible.

My Family: Erik, Brady, and Rylan, you are my constant "why" and my biggest support system. Erik, thank you for your unwavering support of everything I do. You never think my ideas are too wild, or if you do, you support me anyway. We make a great team. Kids, watching you grow up has been the highlight of my life. I love who you both are and who you are both becoming. Thank you for inspiring me to be the best version of myself for you.

To my parents, it was your love of lists and planning that started this whole thing. Thank you for all you have given me over the years and for always being my biggest fan.

Jen. You and I are a waste of flesh and I wouldn't have it anyother way. Thank you for being my person. You inspire me and ground me and make me smile. I know you always have my back and I have yours. I'll never forget that walk we took around the golf course 20 years ago....it started it all.

Everyone needs a business bestie like Leah Neaderthal. Leah, you are my favorite coach and my dear friend. It has been incredible getting to grow these businesses and these babies side-by-side.

And to every client, coach, and teacher I have ever had. You have shaped me and this book in some way. I am constantly learning and I thank you for your contribution to that growth.

Lastly, the work I do at Let's Collective and Focus Sessions, including writing this book, is done on the unceded land of the Me-Wuk (Coast Miwok) peoples, the first inhabitants of the land now known as the Marin Coast, where our headquarters are located.

REFERENCES & RESOURCES

Focus Sessions

Focus Sessions provide unlimited, facilitated virtual co-working. Join us for a distraction-free, science-backed way to create the dedicated time you need to accomplish your most important work.

Try our membership out for free at http://focus-sessions.com. You'll discover it's the most productive 90 minutes of your day.

Books

Below is a list of resources for you to dive further into the topics in this book. These are all sources that have heavily influenced me, my practices, and the content of this book

Burnout: The Secret to Unlocking the Stress Cycle

by Emily Nagoski, Amelia Nagoski, et al.

Indistractable: How to Control Your Attention and Choose Your Life

by Nir Eyal, Julie Li, et al.

The Sweet Spot: How to Accomplish More by Doing Less

by Christine Carter Ph.D.

Atomic Habits: An Easy & Proven Way to Build Good Habits & Break Bad Ones

by James Clear

The 12 Week Year: Get More Done in 12 Weeks than Others Do in 12 Months

by Brian P. Moran, Michael Lennington, et al.

Essentialism: The Disciplined Pursuit of Less

by Greg McKeown

The ONE Thing: The Surprisingly Simple Truth About Extraordinary Results

By Gary Keller

Deep Work: Rules for Focused Success in a Distracted World

by Cal Newport, Jeff Bottoms, et al.

Overwhelmed: How to Work, Love, and Play When No One Has the Time

by Brigid Schulte

You Are a Badass at Making Money: Master the Mindset of Wealth

Jen Sincero

ABOUT THE AUTHOR

Megan Flatt is on a mission to make entrepreneurship easier. She believes you can have a thriving business, a community, and a life — but you don't need more time, you need more focus.

As a Business Growth Strategist, she started Focus Sessions to help entrepreneurs ditch distractions and work more intentionally. She uses science, a solid plan, and a whole lot of Post-it notes to help her clients do their Most Important Work without overwhelm.

Megan's favorite affirmation is "You have exactly the time you need."

Besides helping business owners focus, Megan is obsessed with lattes, office supplies, and romance novels. Outside of work, you can find her focus turned to her husband and two kids, probably near the water, in the San Francisco Bay Area.

You can catch up with Megan at http://focus-sessions.com.

BONUS MATERIALS

To download the resources from this book, scan this code.

Or visit http://focus-sessions.com/bookbonus.

Made in the USA
Las Vegas, NV
13 June 2023